Repentance, covenant, and grace. These connected to the Christian faith but are foreign to so many practicing Christians. Delve into this book to see what the Word of God holds. Compare what you read in this book with what is in the Bible for yourself! You'll find this book to be a helpful resource whether it's your first time picking up a Bible or the thousandth.

Be blessed by this book in the same way it blessed me to write it.

Your brother in the faith, James Boshart

Acknowledgements

This book is written for the express purpose of bringing all glory and honor to my LORD and savior, Jesus the Christ.

I want to thank my wife, Michaella, for being my biggest fan. She has been by my side from the beginning and has always urged me forward through prayerful consideration. She has been my primary editor and I so appreciate the time she has spent helping this book be what it is now. I love her more than words can express.

I want to thank the friends and family, pastors and colleagues, who have been there in my Christian walk, helping me to gain revelation about the rich Word of God. Many of them have eagerly read this book and given me helpful tips and critiques so that it may be where it is now. A big thanks to Donald Richter for challenging me through the whole process to put forth the very best book I can.

I want to thank God Almighty for putting His Word in my hands. The Bible and the revelations He has brought to me about His Word have changed my life and continually lift me up each and every day. As I draw myself to Him, He draws nearer to me; never pushing me away, always guiding me, protecting me, perfecting me, and allowing me to discover more and more the manifold glory that is our God!

Table of Contents:

Introduction & How to Read this Book — pg. 7

What is Repentance? — pg. 15

What is Covenant? — pg. 33

What is Grace? — pg. 61

What is a Christian? — pg. 84

What Now? — pg. 115

Conclusion — pg. 131

Appendix - Tongues, Travailing, and Psalms — pg. 134

Introduction

At about 11 PM on November the 23, 2022, as I was laying down to bed, the LORD prompted me to start writing this book. It had been on my heart to write a book (or a few) for some time but I could sense the book writing itself and I told myself "I'll start in the morning" to which I could almost hear Him say "you can start now."

This book is a culmination of studies that I have been doing over the last year on repentance, repenting, grace, and our appropriate response to each of these. I am not a trained biblical scholar. I have no professional training in the studies of doctrines or dogmas taught in most Christian churches. This book is meant to represent what I found in Scripture and how I sense the LORD is leading me to help others gain a revelation of what it means to repent, what grace truly is, and what we are supposed to do to live a life that we do not actually deserve. I will endeavor to make it clear the translations I use, the source for additional comments, and identify which thoughts and opinions are my own.

As you read, I would ask that you check each and every verse out yourself. I will quote from *The Passion Translation* (TPT), the *New American Study Bible* (NASB), the *King James Version* (KJV), the *Amplified Bible* (AMP), the *New Living Translation* (NLT), the *Aramaic Bible in Plain English*, the *Christian English Version* (CEV), the *Good News Translation* (GNT), the *Literal Standard Version* (LSV), and the *Douay-Rheims Bible* (DRB), as well as the *Berean Standard Bible* (BSB), which will be the primary source of all Bible quotations used in this book. Most reference materials come from the *Passion Translation* footnotes, the *Concordance of the NASB*, *Strong's Concordance*, and *HELPS-Word Studies* (Bible Hub has been a hugely helpful resource for each of these, though the physical copies of *Strong's* and the NASB Concordance reveal different pieces of context and definition not found online).

As I mentioned, I am not a biblical scholar. At the time of writing, I am an Instructional Coach at a charter school in New Mexico. As I completed this book, I have become the assistant principal of middle school at one of our campuses. I have taught for over 4 years in Algebra 2, AP Statistics, PreCalculus, 6th and 7th Grade Mathematics. I went to Tarleton State University in Stephenville, Texas where I completed my degree as a B.S. in Physics, minoring in Mathematics, after graduating high school in Mesquite, Texas. I was raised Catholic, fell out of the faith in college and then hit rock bottom while working at a bar and grill in Albuquerque, NM. However, the LORD was not content with me blaspheming Him and abandoning Him. I want to share with you what the LORD has revealed to me so you may be better equipped for the trials and tribulations that lay ahead.

You may be faced with people who are two-faced and who speak ill of you behind your back despite being sweet to your face. You may be faced with an illness in your mind or in your body. You may find that despite the great and precious promises the Word of God holds, your situation seems to scream the opposite. As you read through this study of the Word, ask yourself what challenges your preconceived notions of what God has in store for you. I pray that you will find that God has a plan for you, a plan that is good and not evil. God is the healer, the redeemer, the provider, and the miracle worker in the face of sickness, oppression, and certain failure. The LORD is a merciful God who ever seeks to bring goodness to your life. You may find as you read through this book that I make some fundamental assumptions about what you know about God, Jesus Christ, the Bible, and the Church as a whole. I apologize if in your reading I say something that appears out of nowhere. I do hope that this text can be enjoyed by those who know little about God as well as those who have walked with Him for a long time. As always, some pieces will be left out as there are a finite number of pages in this book and I am limited in what I can detail in a single book. As the LORD leads me in writing other texts, I hope you find something in any of them that speaks to you on a personal level.

If you gain nothing else from this book, I hope you gain the following:

There is a God who loves you dearly, He has a plan for you and it is so good, the LORD loves all of His people but He will never force you to love Him back, we all deserve eternal damnation but through Jesus we have salvation, and the hope that Jesus has given each of us is a free gift that we have the responsibility of sharing with others. Through Jesus, God has called you back into a relationship with Him, a relationship where He tends to your every need and desire. You are called for a greater purpose in serving the Most High God.

I love you dearly and it is my sincerest hope you are growing more and more in your walk with Jesus today.

James Boshart

How to Read This Book

The Bible

Thank you for taking the time to pursue this study into the Word of God. What is meant by that phrase, "Word of God?" The Bible is a collection of books written by various authors over hundreds of years. More than that, this collection of books is believed to be divinely inspired by God Himself. Despite the separation of time, space, and author, the books often have very clear threads connecting them, pointing to a greater truth that identifies who God is.

The Bible is made of two major parts: the Old Testament and the New Testament (we will dig into those names later). The Old Testament can be thought of as the Hebrew Bible for two reasons, 1) it was originally written in Hebrew and 2) it is a collection of books that Jews even today acknowledge with validity. The New Testament was written in the "world language" at the time which was Greek, even though Latin was starting to take the stage as Rome had been in power for quite some time. In fact, the Hebrew Bible is actually translated from Hebrew into Greek prior to the writing of any of the New Testament books (called the Septuagint).

In the Old Testament, the first five books (Genesis, Exodus, Leviticus, Numbers, and Deuteronomy) pertain to what is called "the Law" (referred to as the "Torah" or the "Pentateuch"). God gave Moses a revelation about the origin of man, covenant with God, and the history leading to that revelation. Moses, in addition to writing these books, actually wrote some of the Psalms as well. Much of these first five books are very literal (very clear sequences of events, lists of names) while other parts seem to tell of a larger picture that each of us must have revealed to us (in the creation narrative in Genesis, it seems as though a series of events are listed and then the author goes back to retell some of those parts more in depth). The next few books (Joshua, Judges, Ruth, First and Second Samuel, First and Second Kings, First and Second Chronicles, Ezra, Nehemiah, and Esther) are historical in nature. These books very much tell the story of the Israelite people in their successes and in their hardships. We see that cataloging of idolatrous worship, early prophets, and some of the greatest rulers of the "known world" at that time. Then are the books of poetry: Job, Psalms, Proverbs, Ecclesiastes, Song of Solomon, and (skipping a couple books) Lamentations. A lot of figurative language is used through these books as well as some of the best descriptions of the mercy and power of God. The last portion is pertaining to the prophets: Ezekiel, Daniel, Hosea, Joel, Amos, Obadiah, Jonah, Micah, Nahum, Habakkuk, Zephaniah, Haggai, Zechariah, and Malachi. These books contain very useful historical information as well as prophetic messages, a message pertaining to the people of the time but also was timeless and would apply to other people at another time (we will talk about prophecy later in this book). The Old Testament was *for* the Jewish people so when it is read, it must be read through that lens. All throughout the Old Testament, however, there was a pointing to the coming of a Messiah, a Savior: Jesus.

The New Testament, much smaller, is made up of the Gospel and Acts of the Apostles: Matthew, Mark, Luke, John, and Acts. Acts does not count as part of the Gospel but it does show the last message of Jesus to His disciples and their work spreading the message of Jesus to the world. These books share the personal encounter of Jesus and the early start of the church. Much of the rest of the New Testament is referred to as "epistles" or letters to the churches: Romans, First and Second Corinthians, Galatians, Ephesians, Philippians, Colossians, First and Second Thessalonians, First and Second Timothy, Titus, Philemon, Hebrews, James, First and Second Peter, First, Second, and Third John, and Jude. These books were written to real churches who were struggling with real issues. These books are as much for you today as it was for them (though the context of *who* the message was written and *why* the message was written is very important to keep in mind). The last book of the Bible is called Revelation and it is prophetic in nature. Some of it can be interpreted as very literal, some of it seems to be a message in a spiritual sense. Do not discount the reading of Revelation because within it are seven letters to seven churches, much like the other epistles. This book warns of "not forsaking your first love" and to not be "luke-warm" in your faith. The New Testament is for those who desire a deep understanding of Jesus. The Old Testament reveals Jesus and God's desire for a relationship with us, but it can be easy to get bogged down with statements about "the Law" if we do not understand who Jesus is or why He came.

There are other "extra-biblical" books that some people include in their Bibles, often referred to as "apocrypha" or "hidden" books: Tobit, Judith, First and Second Maccabees, Baruch, Esdras, Prayer of Manasseh, and others. There are also books like the book of Enoch and texts found as part of the "Dead Sea Scrolls." For one reason or another (inability to prove authenticity, peculiarities like the language it was written in, appearing to be written in a significantly different time period than comparable texts), early leaders of the church did not ultimately agree to keep these books in the Bible (though some denominations like Greek Orthodox and Roman Catholic contain some of these books). There are quite a few interesting books on the history of developing the Bible as it is today (referred to as the "canon"), this not that book. These books will not be used as references nor will they be mentioned again in this book. As far as this book is concerned, they are not a part of the Bible and therefore not a part of this study.

One must note some fundamental assumptions that will be used throughout this book: the Bible is real, the Bible is true, and the Bible is trustworthy. We will not take the time here to dig into each of these but it is absolutely necessary that as I write this book, I take the Bible to be a collection of words God had man write so we would know Him better. I will sometimes refer to the Bible as "Scriptures," "the Word of God," or simply "the Word." If you are to develop a relationship with the Father God, you must accept the Bible as true and you must spend time with it.

As was mentioned in the introduction, various translations are used. This is for a few reasons: 1) the original scrolls that make up the Bible were written in Hebrew and Greek and my understanding of both is very limited, and 2) since the Bible was originally written in a different language, some things are missed in a transliteration (like the King James Version or the Berean Standard Bible) so other possible translations of the same original word can reveal more about the message and usage of that word. The Hebrew and Greek languages are rich and beautiful languages and assuming that when we read our Bible in part without taking the time to understand the message brought by each word, we allow ourselves to miss the bigger picture. It is my hope that rather than cause you to challenge and cast aside the Bible that this study helps bring you to revere and respect the Bible as the complex, powerful, and living Word of God.

Reference Text and Translations

Throughout this book, you will see reference to Strong's Concordance, NAS (New American Standard) Exhaustive Concordance (copyright 1981, 1998 by The Lockman Foundation, all rights reserved Lockman.org), and HELPS Word-studies (copyright 2021 by The Discovery Bible, discoverybible.com). Strong's Concordance, originally written by James Strong in 1890, is generally recognized as the most used biblical reference tool. By indexing each word from the KJV (King James Version), it is possible to connect the English words back to their root word found in Aramaic/Hebrew from the Old Testament or Greek from the New Testament. Similarly, the Lockman Foundation published the New American Standard Translation of the Bible and an accompanying concordance to best support literal word-for-word translation originally in 1971 but have sent reprinted and given minor text edits.

While both concordances are strong reference tools, Strong's is the most widely used because of the numerical coding system in place. There are over 8,600 Hebrew and over 5,600 Greek root words given a reference number. An example used in the first chapter of this book is G3340 *metanoéō*. The G in the front denotes a Greek root word with the number corresponding to an alphabetically organized list of words (the 3340th word in the list). This is included so the reader can see for themselves the roots of words discussed, enough context such that reference material does not need to be sought but also enough information that any student of the Word can investigate the claims and connections found within this book. Another example is given as H5146 *Noach* נֹחַ, where the H in this case is given to indicate a Hebrew root word. When possible, the original Hebrew and Greek characters are included. This inclusion is meant to remind the reader that the Bible as we read it today comes from an original source which is not written in English.

In comparing translations, it is important to consider the motivation of the translators. The KJV, while a literal translation, was published with the intent of identifying the clergy as essential to best support the Catholic Church. The Revised Standard Version (RSV) was put out as a means of opposing that view and is often seen as a more "liberal translation." Regardless of the intentions of the writers of various translations, this book is meant to provide comparison and invoke powerful imagery with regards to both the original language and the context in which it was written. Let us look at a common verse, John 3:16, in a few different translations that will be used in this book:

KJV- "For God so loved the world, that he gave his only begotten Son, that whosoever believeth in him should not perish, but have everlasting life."

Amplified- "For God so [greatly] loved *and* dearly prized the world, that He [even] gave His [One and] only begotten Son, so that whoever believes *and* trusts in Him [as Savior] shall not perish, but have eternal life."

New Living Translation (NLT)- "For this is how God loved the world: He gave his one and only Son, so that everyone who believes in him will not perish but have eternal life."

The Passion Translation- "For this is how much God loved the world - he gave his one and only, unique Son *as a gift*. So now everyone who believes in him will never perish but experience everlasting life."

While the message is the same, the wording is subtly different. It is very important to keep this in mind because wrong teaching and incorrect doctrine can be created by the usage of an English word that is not actually present or intended from the Hebrew or Greek. As the reader, you will have to make decisions about how you interpret what you read.
Another poignant example, also from John's Gospel, pertains to the usage of two different Greek words for "love" that are translated the same. John 21:16 is seen in a few different translations as:

BSB- Jesus asked a second time, "Simon son of John, do you love Me?" "Yes, Lord," he answered, "You know I love You." Jesus told him, "Shepherd My sheep."

KJV- He said to him again a second time, "Simon, *son* of Jonah, do you love Me?" He said to Him, "Yes, Lord; You know that I love You." He said to him, "Tend My sheep."

New International Version (NIV)- Again Jesus said, "Simon son of John, do you love me?" He answered, "Yes, Lord, you know that I love you." Jesus said, "Take care of my sheep."

Amplified- Again He said to him a second time, "Simon, *son* of John, do you love Me [with total commitment and devotion]?" He said to Him, "Yes, Lord; You know that I love You [with a deep, personal affection, as for a close friend]." Jesus said to him, "Shepherd My sheep."

Notice that the first three translations listed here use the word "love" but the Amplified gives two different statements in brackets. The reason being is that when Jesus says "love," He says "*agape*." When Simon (Peter) responds, he says "*phileo*." Different words, slightly different meanings.

Assuming that one singular translation will adequately say what is in the original language is a false assumption. That is not to say most students of the Word do not have a preferred translation to read, but that a close reading of the text identifying both context and the original word used are important (for more on context, see the section on the Corinthian church in Chapter 19).

What is Repentance?

Chapter 1 - First Mention of Repent/Repentance in the New Testament

> In those days John the Baptist came, preaching in the wilderness of Judea and saying, "**Repent**, for the kingdom of heaven is near." This is he who was spoken of through the prophet Isaiah:
>
> "A voice of one calling in the wilderness,
> 'Prepare the way for the Lord,
> make straight paths for Him.' "
>
> … But when John saw many of the Pharisees and Sadducees coming to his place of baptism, he said to them, "You brood of vipers, who warned you to flee from the coming wrath? Produce fruit, then, in keeping with **repentance**. And do not presume to say to yourselves, 'We have Abraham as our father.' For I tell you that out of these stones God can raise up children for Abraham. The ax lies ready at the root of the trees, and every tree that does not produce good fruit will be cut down and thrown into the fire.
>
> I baptize you with water for **repentance**, but after me will come One more powerful than I, whose sandals I am not worthy to carry. He will baptize you with the Holy Spirit and with fire. His winnowing fork is in His hand to clear His threshing floor and to gather His wheat into the barn; but He will burn up the chaff with unquenchable fire."
>
> - Matthew 3:1-3, 7-12 Berean Standard Bible (BSB)

John the Baptist helps to provide a definition for "repent" and "repentance" as well as prophesy about what it is Jesus will do in the future. It is noteworthy that this is the first mention in the New Testament for the words "repent" and "repentance." Many biblical scholars agree that the context in which a word is mentioned in the Bible helps to define that word. The phrase "Repent, for the kingdom of heaven is near" is also seen in the next chapter spoken by Jesus after the imprisonment of John the Baptist (Matthew 4:12,17, BSB):

> When Jesus heard that John had been imprisoned, He withdrew to Galilee… From that time on Jesus began to preach, "Repent, for the kingdom of heaven is near."

After John first proclaims "repent," there is a verse given from Isaiah 40:3 (BSB). "Prepare the way for the LORD, make straight paths for Him." [See also Luke 3:3-6 (BSB).] This is what follows the very first mention of the word "repent" so we can use this as a means of defining the word. John the Baptist is suggesting that to repent is preparing the way for the LORD by making straight paths for Him. It is hard to get lost on a straight path because one can see ahead down that path. In fact, Isaiah 40:4 (BSB) goes the step further by saying *"Every valley shall be filled in, and every mountain and hill shall be brought low. All the crooked ways shall become straight, and the rough places plains."* Not only are the paths made straight, but level. When traveling down a straight and level path, one can see for miles. Proverbs 15:21 (BSB) reminds us "Folly is joy to one who lacks judgment, but a man of understanding walks a straight path." So those who repent, those that make a level, straight path, must be men and women of understanding.

In Greek, the word used for "repent" is conjugated from μετανοέω or '*metanoeó*.' Strong's Concordance defines the word as "to change one's mind or purpose" and HELPS Word-studies gives: G3340 *metanoéō* (from 3326 /*metá*, "*changed after* being *with*" and 3539 /*noiéō*, "think") – properly, "*think* differently *after*," "after a change of *mind*"; to *repent* (literally, "*think* differently *after*wards"). We could think about this as changing not in word only, but also in deed. To repent therefore becomes much greater than a simple "I'm sorry," but instead a change in how we are thinking and acting. In repenting of lying, our thoughts should no longer plan lies. In repenting of sexual sins, our thoughts should move away from such sins. In repenting of idolatry and putting other things or people before God, our thoughts should then move towards putting God first. We are to repent not only from sinful acts but from "dead works," this endeavoring to earn God's goodness. This competition of "who is holier?" is a sin in and of itself, a sin we will look at through the lives of the religious leaders of Jesus' day. To repent does not mean you are perfect now, but it does mean a departure from an old way of thinking.

The word "repent" certainly brings with it the idea of change. Look back at Matthew 3:7-8 (BSB), where John the Baptist says "You brood of vipers, who warned you to flee from the coming wrath? Produce fruit, then, in keeping with repentance..." If one repents (and truly repents) there must be fruit, some outward expression that shows a change. If one does not repent, there is a coming wrath. In the Greek, the word used for repentance is from μετάνοια or '*metanoia*,' similar to the word for repent above. John the Baptist is warning the religious leaders of the day not to repent in word only but that a change in their thinking must occur as well.

Chapter 2 - Repent/Repentance in the Old Testament

In the Hebrew, the word for "repent" is נחם or *'nacham'* which is defined by Strong's Exhaustive Concordance as comfort self, ease one's self, repent.
A primitive root; properly, to sigh, i.e. Breathe strongly; by implication, to be sorry, i.e. (in a favorable sense) to pity, console or (reflexively) rue; or (unfavorably) to avenge (oneself) -- comfort (self), ease (one's self), repent(-er,-ing, self).

Keeping in mind that the first mention of a word helps to define that word, the first mention in the Bible for *'nacham'* goes back to Genesis and the story of Noah. Taking Genesis 5:29 (BSB), 'And he named him Noah,e saying, "May this one comfort us in the labor and toil of our hands caused by the ground that the LORD has cursed." ' The footnote beside the name Noah is "e *Noah* sounds like the Hebrew for *rest* or *comfort*." So then our three words in Hebrew are:

> Noah - H5146 *Noach* נֹחַ
> Rest - H5117 *nuach* נוּחַ
> Repent/Comforted - H5162 *nacham* נחם

As Genesis chapter 6 opens up, we see that the sins of man are such that it catches the attention of the LORD. In the King James Version (KJV), verses 5-7 read,

> And GOD saw that the wickedness of man *was* great in the earth, and *that* every imagination of the thoughts of his heart *was* only evil continually. And it **repented** the LORD that He had made man on the earth, and it grieved Him at His heart. And the LORD said, "I will destroy man whom I have created from the face of the earth; both man, and beast, and the creeping thing, and the fowls of the air; for it **repenteth** Me that I have made them."

When mankind was given the free will to make their own choices, as a collective group, they chose poorly. In fact, it was such that the hearts and minds of all of the people were "evil continually." Going back to the visual and descriptive definition of repent as a deep sigh, it puts an image in your mind of God looking down on His creation (a creation a few chapters back He called "good") as a father who looks at his children who not only made a poor choice but are actively living in sin. You can almost hear Him sigh in disapproval. We see that this word really builds on the word "grieve" that is used, implying that seeing mankind in the state it was in was dissatisfying to the LORD.

Now that same word carries a different meaning in a different context. Consider Job 42:1-6 (BSB):

> Then Job replied to the LORD:
>
> "I know that You can do all things
> and that no plan of Yours can be thwarted.
> You asked, 'Who is this
> who conceals My counsel without knowledge?'
> Surely I spoke of things I did not understand,
> things too wonderful for me to know.
> You said, 'Listen now, and I will speak.
> I will question you, and you shall inform Me.'
> My ears had heard of You,
> but now my eyes have seen You.
> Therefore I retract my words,
> and I **repent** in dust and ashes."

Job, realizing the errors in his words against God, retracts his words as part of his repentance. Though this is the same word, the meaning is different. Here the phrase "retract my words" becomes the defining phrase for repent in this case. Connect this back to a commonly quoted Scripture by both opponents and proponents of the Bible, 1 Samuel 15:29 (BSB), "Moreover, the Glory of Israel does not lie or **change His mind**, for He is not a man, that He should **change His mind**." The bolded phrase "change His mind" is that same word "nacham" cited above in Job and Genesis. Many Christians have this verse memorized for it verifies the truth about God that He is the same yesterday, today, and forevermore (Hebrews 13:8 (KJV) says "Jesus Christ the same yesterday, and today, and forever," Malachi 3:6 (KJV) says "For I *am* the LORD, I do not change..." James 1:17 (BSB) says "Every good and perfect gift is from above, coming down from the Father of the heavenly lights, with whom there is no change or shifting shadow.") and yet this same verse seems to contradict Genesis 6:6-7. Why?

True revelation of this verse relies upon the phrase "the Glory of Israel does not lie." Before Samuel gives us the verse mentioned in chapter 15, verse 29, he is speaking with the LORD. In 1 Samuel 15:11 (BSB), the LORD tells Samuel, "I **regret** that I have made Saul king, for he has turned away from following Me and has not carried out My instructions." Regret? Why would the LORD regret (that same word used for repent) of His actions? To answer that, we need a bit of context for what is written in 1 Samuel 15.

Saul is the first king of the Israelites though originally, as was dictated by God, the Israelites had judges that ruled over them. However, the people demanded they have a king like the other nations. 1 Samuel 8:6-9 (BSB), reads:

But when they said, "Give us a king to judge us," their demand was displeasing in the sight of Samuel; so he prayed to the LORD.

And the LORD said to Samuel, "Listen to the voice of the people in all that they say to you. For it is not you they have rejected, but they have rejected Me as their king. Just as they have done from the day I brought them up out of Egypt until this day, forsaking Me and serving other gods, so they are doing to you. Now listen to them, but you must solemnly warn them and show them the manner of the king who will reign over them."

So we see that it was not God's desire to appoint a king. Again, 1 Samuel 15:11, "I **regret** that I have made Saul king, for he has turned away from following Me and has not carried out My instructions" connects to the sin of disobedience much in the same way the Israelites turned away from God after they fled Egypt. This use of "regret" helps to highlight that our actions that require repentance affect God. Saul ultimately did repent and beg forgiveness, but not until after Samuel told Saul that the consequence for disobedience would be Saul's removal as king.

God does not change His mind. He does not make mistakes. He did create humans who make choices that many times are outside of what God has in mind for us (properly, His Will for us) and in these cases (e.g., mankind at the time of the great flood, Saul after disobeying the LORD) Scripture mentions that God would "repent". It would be more appropriate for us to read these verses in acknowledging that any time we see God repenting that we read it as "the actions of man grieved the LORD" in that in each and every case it is not the LORD who needs to change, but the wicked misdeeds of man that do.

Chapter 3 - Examining Repentance Through the Ministry of Jesus

In Matthew 4, Jesus preaches a message much like the one John the Baptist preached. When John the Baptist is imprisoned in Matthew 11, Jesus had been preaching and teaching for some time so He was able to see if, like John the Baptist cautioned the Pharisees and Sadducees, the people had fruit to show their repentance. Starting in chapter 11, verse 21 in the BSB, Jesus says:

> "Woe to you, Chorazin! Woe to you, Bethsaida! For if the miracles that were performed in you had been performed in Tyre and Sidon, they would have repented long ago in sackcloth and ashes. But I tell you, it will be more bearable for Tyre and Sidon on the day of judgment than for you.

> And you, Capernaum, will you be lifted up to heaven? No, you will be brought down to Hades! For if the miracles that were performed in you had been performed in Sodom, it would have remained to this day. But I tell you that it will be more bearable for Sodom on the day of judgment than for you."

Jesus preaches and teaches in the regions of Chorazin, Bethsaida, and Capernaum, performing many miracles as He does, and yet "it will be more bearable for" Tyre and Sidon or Sodom than these regions on the day of judgment. Tyre and Sidon as well as Sodom are places from the Old Testament that received condemning judgment from the LORD through the prophets. As recorded by Joel and Ezekiel, the sins each committed are as follows:

Joel 3:4-6 (BSB): "Now what do you have against Me, O Tyre, Sidon, and all the regions of Philistia? Are you rendering against Me a recompense? If you retaliate against Me, I will swiftly and speedily return your recompense upon your heads. For you took My silver and gold and carried off My finest treasures to your temples. You sold the people of Judah and Jerusalem to the Greeks, to send them far from their homeland."

Ezekiel 16:49-50, Amplified Bible (AMP): "Behold, this was the sin of your sister Sodom: she and her daughters (outlying cities) had arrogance, abundant food, and careless ease, but she did not help the poor and needy. They were haughty and committed repulsive acts before Me; therefore I removed them when I saw it."

Despite the sins done in Tyre, Sidon, and Sodom, Jesus proclaims, "it will be more bearable ... on the day of judgment" for them than it would be for Chorazin, Bethsaida, and Capernaum. The reason for this severe judgment is given in the verse prior to Jesus speaking in Matthew 11:20 (BSB), 'Then Jesus began to denounce the cities in which most of His miracles had been performed, because they did not repent.' A very clear judgment for an unrepentant group of people. It is important to note that there is not a comparison of sins here (whose sin is greater) but rather that there is punishment for sin. Considering His audience, Jesus was talking to Jews who would have known the blessings and curses given in Deuteronomy 28, blessing for those who followed the Word of God and curse for those who would live outside the Will of God by refusing His Word. These blessings and curses come before the Levitical law which gives the Jews exact one-for-one correspondence for how to deal with sins. The curses in Deuteronomy, however, are subject to anyone who lives in a life of sin, whether purposefully by actively ignoring or challenging God or by ignorance of the Word of God. Jesus' point here is that sin results in consequence. Paul's revelation of this is seen in Romans 6:23 (BSB), "For the wages of sin is death…"

The Gospel according to Luke holds more for us on this topic of repentance. In Luke 11:29-32 (BSB), it is written:

> As the crowds were increasing, Jesus said, "This is a wicked generation. It demands a sign, but none will be given it except the sign of Jonah. For as Jonah was a sign to the Ninevites, so the Son of Man will be a sign to this generation.
>
> The Queen of the South will rise at the judgment with the men of this generation and condemn them; for she came from the ends of the earth to hear the wisdom of Solomon, and now One greater than Solomon is here. The men of Nineveh will stand at the judgment with this generation and condemn it; for they repented at the preaching of Jonah, and now One greater than Jonah is here."

Much like before, there was a comparison made between the people of His day and those from the Old Testament. The Ninevites, however, are important because as the enemy of the Israelite people, they faced judgment. God sent Jonah who (begrudgingly) went and prophesied to them about their coming destruction. After hearing his words, the people repented! The people of Nineveh are important to consider because they did not attack Jonah (the Bible is full of examples of people attacking God's chosen messenger) but instead they believed the words he said were true.

Jesus' words from Luke were spoken as a response to what was recorded above in Luke 11:14-16 (BSB),

> One day Jesus was driving out a demon that was mute. And when the demon was gone, the man who had been mute spoke. The crowds were amazed, but some of them said, "It is by Beelzebul, the prince of the demons, that He drives out demons." And others tested Him by demanding a sign from heaven.

The actions of these people are that of a people who are obstinate and defiant, not a people repentant of their sins. Despite the fact that Jesus is working miracles, many cannot receive His message because it opposes their religion. The religious leaders of that day taught the letter of the law and hyper-focused on the actions of a person while Jesus taught on the intention of the law, the Heart of God. It is important to distinguish the teaching of Jesus from religious teaching of the day because in many points, they sounded the same. So in what way were they different, even to the point that the religious leaders and Pharisees wanted to kill Jesus? Luke 11:37-52 (BSB), records the interaction between Jesus and the religious leaders at a dinner that can help illuminate this contrast between Jesus and the religious (similarly in Matthew 23):

> As Jesus was speaking, a Pharisee invited Him to dine with him; so He went in and reclined at the table. But the Pharisee was surprised to see that Jesus did not first wash before the meal.

[Note: The ritual of hand washing created a point of contention between Jesus and the others.]

> "Now then," said the Lord, "you Pharisees clean the outside of the cup and dish, but inside you are full of greed and wickedness. You fools! Did not the One who made the outside make the inside as well? But give as alms the things that are within you, and you will see that everything is clean for you.

[Note: Our definition for repent refers to a change in the mind. Jesus here gives the comparison of inward and outward cleanliness to help exemplify that point.]

> Woe to you Pharisees! You pay tithes of mint, rue, and every herb, but you disregard justice and the love of God. You should have practiced the latter without neglecting the former.

[Note: Jesus does not condemn the Pharisees for tithing, but He does correct them that tithing without demonstrating justice and love to God is not what the law intends.]

> Woe to you Pharisees! You love the chief seats in the synagogues and the greetings in the marketplaces. Woe to you! For you are like unmarked graves, which men walk over without even noticing."

[Note: Jesus corrects the Pharisees about the importance they have been placing upon themselves. Our actions should bring glory and honor to God, not to bring attention to ourselves.]

> One of the experts in the law told Him, "Teacher, when You say these things, You insult us as well."
>
> "Woe to you as well, experts in the law!" He replied. "You weigh men down with heavy burdens, but you yourselves will not lift a finger to lighten their load.

[Note: Compare this to Matthew 23:4 and 23:15 where Jesus charges that though these teachers of the law endeavor to bring people to God, their wrong teaching (hyper-fixating on the letter of the law and not its intent) has caused a negative condition for the people.]

> Woe to you! You build tombs for the prophets, but it was your fathers who killed them. So you are witnesses consenting to the deeds of your fathers: They killed the prophets, and you build their tombs. Because of this, the wisdom of God said, 'I will send them prophets and apostles; some of them they will kill and others they will persecute.'

[Note: Just like the prophets of the Old Testament, both John the Baptist and Jesus come preaching that the people must change their ways and yet, in the end, these two share the same fate by being killed by the people who desperately need their message.]

> As a result, this generation will be charged with the blood of all the prophets that has been shed since the foundation of the world, from the blood of Abel to the blood of Zechariah, who was killed between the altar and the sanctuary. Yes, I tell you, all of it will be charged to this generation.

[Note: Why charge an entire generation? Jesus in the above comparison is not simply looking at the outward acts, the act of sinning itself, but the heart condition of the people. This is a group of people who are refusing to acknowledge they have done anything wrong. What a time there is for repentance when we think we are the ones in the right!]

> Woe to you experts in the law! For you have taken away the key to knowledge. You yourselves have not entered, and you have hindered those who were entering."

[Note: What a serious charge! These religious teachers of that day have "hindered those who are entering." Compare this to Malachi 2:8 and Micah 3:5-6. Also, see the judgment Jesus gives over one whose teaching would cause a young believer in Christ to fall away from Him in Matthew 18:6]

Jesus connects their sins with those that came before them. Looking at Matthew 5:19-20 (BSB), Jesus condemns the Pharisees by saying "So then, whoever breaks one of the least of these commandments and teaches others to do likewise will be called least in the kingdom of heaven; but whoever practices and teaches them will be called great in the kingdom of heaven. For I tell you that unless your righteousness exceeds that of the scribes and Pharisees, you will never enter the kingdom of heaven." How much more clear can you get: whoever practices and teaches them [the commandments] will be called great in the kingdom of heaven. These religious leaders who were tasked with teaching the Law found themselves contradicting it because, as Jesus stated in Luke 11, they were more in love with the appearance of righteousness as opposed to doing the right thing. This shows us the error of religious leaders across all time: when you focus on appearing to do good but you do not set your mind and heart with the attitude of doing good, your ways are in error. The Pharisees have not given thought to the condition of the heart, nor the motivation of why the Law is in place. These religious "elite" were too busy practicing the "works of the Law" to know the heart and intention of the Law. There was not a specific ordinance that was broken that these men needed to repent of, rather they needed to repent of their actions, the "dead works" that they believed in so strongly. Consider a lawyer that swindles people by loopholes in contracts. His actions may be in line with the law (thus, "appearing righteous") but in actuality, his actions only serve him and hurt others. Or consider an organization that claims to be "humanitarian" or "non-profit" with a mission to help others. This organization has a fund-raiser where long-time partners and other individuals donate thousands or millions of dollars to support the mission of the organization. If the organization then takes that money and funds a political campaign, there may be no legal misdeed. If the donors, however, do not support that politician, there has been a misleading of the people in the name of a "greater good." A person or organization that would do that is no better than the Pharisees of Jesus' day.

How many times have we spoken ill of someone who has spoken a lie or stolen something? How many times have we demonstrated a righteous indignation towards those who have sinned while not examining the sin in our own lives (particularly of arrogance and pride)? How important it is for us to examine our lives much in the way Jesus spoke in His Sermon on the Mount in Matthew 7:4 (BSB) where He said, "How can you say to your brother, 'Let me take the speck out of your eye,' while there is still a beam in your own eye?" Let us take to examining our own thoughts, actions, and posture before extending our "helpful" comments to others in error.

A discussion arises in Luke 13:1-8 (BSB), that speaks more on the comparison of sins:

> At that time some of those present told Jesus about the Galileans whose blood Pilate had mixed with their sacrifices. To this He replied, "Do you think that these Galileans were worse sinners than all the other Galileans, because they suffered this fate? No, I tell you. But unless you repent, you too will all perish. Or those eighteen who were killed when the tower of Siloam collapsed on them: Do you

> think that they were more sinful than all the others living in Jerusalem? No, I tell you. But unless you repent, you too will all perish."

[Note: Jesus tells us directly that destruction is not prioritized based on sin. This would have produced some contention among the Jews at the time because of their understanding of different classifications of sin. Exodus 34:7 gives three words for wrongdoing: '*chatta'ah,*' '*pesha,*' and '*avon,*' for "sin," "transgression," and "iniquity." Jesus does not make the distinction here. He does not dig into the type of sin or the weight of the consequence of that sin. Instead, He lumps all of sin together. We have all sinned and unless we repent, destruction will seek us out. For in-depth examples of the rewards for living in the will of God or consequences for living outside the will of God, read Deuteronomy chapter 28, noting in particular what is deemed "blessing" and what is a "curse." We must shake off this perception that "God's going to get you" but understand instead that a law of the universe is that there are consequences for each action.]

> Then Jesus told this parable: "A man had a fig tree that was planted in his vineyard. He went to look for fruit on it, but did not find any. So he said to the keeper of the vineyard, 'Look, for the past three years I have come to search for fruit on this fig tree and haven't found any. Therefore cut it down! Why should it use up the soil?'
>
> 'Sir,' the man replied, 'leave it alone again this year, until I dig around it and fertilize it. If it bears fruit next year, fine. But if not, you can cut it down.'"

Notice how the gardener looks to see what kind of fruit the tree is bringing forth and finds nothing. Are we bringing forth fruit that brings honor and glory to God? Are we living a life that brings people to want to know our LORD and Savior? How do I know if the way I live my life brings forth fruit that is pleasing to the LORD? Let us dig deeper into "sin."

Chapter 4 - Who is a Sinner?

In what is referred to as the "Sermon on the Mount," Jesus preaches a message that clears up misconceptions people may have about the Law and what governs sin. As we read through this, examine for yourself: how is Jesus defining sin and does that agree or disagree with how you have been taught. We should be careful to base our understanding of biblical concepts through what is written in the Bible. In Matthew 5, verses 21-48 (BSB), Jesus said:

> "You have heard that it was said to the ancients, 'Do not murder' and 'Anyone who murders will be subject to judgment.' **But I tell you** that anyone who is angry with his brother will be subject to judgment. Again, anyone who says to his brother, 'Raca [fool],' will be subject to the Sanhedrin. But anyone who says, 'You fool!' will be subject to the fire of hell.
>
> So if you are offering your gift at the altar and there remember that your brother has something against you, leave your gift there before the altar. First go and be reconciled to your brother; then come and offer your gift.
>
> Reconcile quickly with your adversary, while you are still on the way to court. Otherwise, he may hand you over to the judge, and the judge may hand you over to the officer, and you may be thrown into prison. **Truly I tell you**, you will not get out until you have paid the last penny.
>
> You have heard that it was said, 'Do not commit adultery.' **But I tell you** that anyone who looks at a woman to lust after her has already committed adultery with her in his heart. If your right eye causes you to sin, gouge it out and throw it away. It is better for you to lose one part of your body than for your whole body to be thrown into hell. And if your right hand causes you to sin, cut it off and throw it away. It is better for you to lose one part of your body than for your whole body to depart into hell.
>
> It has also been said, 'Whoever divorces his wife must give her a certificate of divorce.' **But I tell you** that anyone who divorces his wife, except for sexual immorality, brings adultery upon her. And he who marries a divorced woman commits adultery.
>
> Again, you have heard that it was said to the ancients, 'Do not break your oath, but fulfill your vows to the Lord. **But I tell you** not to swear at all: either by heaven, for it is God's throne; or by the earth, for it is His footstool; or by Jerusalem, for it is the city of the great King. Nor should you swear by your head, for you cannot make

a single hair white or black. Simply let your 'Yes' be 'Yes,' and your 'No,' 'No.' Anything more comes from the evil one.

You have heard that it was said, 'Eye for eye and tooth for tooth.' **But I tell you** not to resist an evil person. If someone slaps you on your right cheek, turn to him the other also; if someone wants to sue you and take your tunic, let him have your cloak as well; and if someone forces you to go one mile, go with him two miles. Give to the one who asks you, and do not turn away from the one who wants to borrow from you.

You have heard that it was said, 'Love your neighbor' and 'Hate your enemy.' **But I tell you**, love your enemies and pray for those who persecute you, that you may be sons of your Father in heaven. He causes His sun to rise on the evil and the good, and sends rain on the righteous and the unrighteous. If you love those who love you, what reward will you get? Do not even tax collectors do the same? And if you greet only your brothers, what are you doing more than others? Do not even Gentiles do the same?

Be perfect, therefore, as your heavenly Father is perfect."

As we dig a bit into what Jesus spoke, notice what others have said and compare to what He says. Books have been and can continue to be written just on what Jesus outlines in this sermon. What I want to bring up is the way in which Jesus shows 1) that the heart and mind of a person committing sin must be considered and 2) the severity of consequences is greater than understood by the people Jesus was teaching. Look specifically at what Jesus says in verses 46 and 47, "If you love those who love you, what reward will you get? Do not even tax collectors do the same? And if you greet only your brothers, what are you doing more than others? Do not even Gentiles do the same?" Jesus is calling the people to be wholly different than what they were before. The call to repentance is not a small, indiscernible change but should be such an apparent change that people around you could not mistake you for anything other than a follower of Christ. It is important to note that the tax collectors would have been Jews that decided to serve the oppressive Roman empire. The tax collector was the most loathed among the Jewish people and was seen as traitorous.

Notice also the very last verse above in which we are called to be "perfect." The word "be" that starts the sentence is in the future tense, indicating that you "will be" (and most certainly "can be"). The AMP gives the verse as, "You, therefore, will be perfect [growing into spiritual maturity both in mind and character, actively integrating godly values into your daily life], as your heavenly Father is perfect." This implies not a single act of turning to God but a continual action.

In his writing to the Church in Rome, Paul wrote the following in Romans 2:4-8 (TPT),

> Do the riches of His extraordinary kindness make you take Him for granted and despise Him? Haven't you experienced how kind and understanding He has been to you? Don't mistake His tolerance for acceptance. Do you realize that all the wealth of His extravagant kindness is meant to melt your heart and lead you into repentance? But because of your calloused heart and refusal to change direction, you are piling up wrath for yourself in the day of wrath, when God's righteous judgment is revealed. For: 'He will give to each one in return for what he has done.' For those living in constant goodness and doing what pleases Him, seeking an unfading glory and honor and imperishable virtue, will experience eternal life. But those governed by selfishness and self-promotion, whose hearts are unresponsive to God's truth and would rather embrace unrighteousness, will experience the fullness of wrath.

Notice the words "melt your heart and lead you to repentance." The LORD can not force someone to repent, but He can lead you to it. In the end, the decision is yours. Notice the way the next sentence starts, "But because of your calloused heart and refusal to change direction…" We see that the unrepentant have a heart condition, they have hardened their hearts. Those who refuse to repent refuse to grow. They shut themselves off from wisdom and refuse to let their hearts be changed. As such, they do not change their path. The unrepentant refuse to change direction. There is a blind charging forward for those who hold onto past wrongs and refuse to repent. May these verses cause us to reflect on our own lives, examining where we have hardened our hearts or become unmoving in the direction we go. We can not be led by God if we are unrepentant or unforgiving.

Consider Romans 12:2 (BSB), "Do not be conformed to this world, but be transformed by the **renewing of your mind**. Then you will be able to test and approve what is the good, pleasing, and perfect will of God." In this verse, Paul, by revelation through the Holy Spirit, is reminding us as Christ followers to renew our mind and not conform ourselves to the world around us. Moreover, the tensing in the Greek implies a continual renewing, an act that must be done over and over and over. How important it is that we must continually realign ourselves with the will of God by analyzing our thoughts and our emotions and comparing them with what the Word of God tells us.

Chapter 5 - Get Your Mind Right

Paul would write in his letter to the Ephesians (4:17-24, BSB) how the followers of Christ should live:

> So I tell you this, and insist on it in the Lord, that you must no longer walk as the Gentiles do, in the futility of their thinking. They are darkened in their understanding and alienated from the life of God because of the ignorance that is in them due to the hardness of their hearts. Having lost all sense of shame, they have given themselves over to sensuality for the practice of every kind of impurity, with a craving for more.

> But this is not the way you came to know Christ. Surely you heard of Him and were taught in Him—in keeping with the truth that is in Jesus— to put off your former way of life, your old self, which is being corrupted by its deceitful desires; to be renewed in the spirit of your minds; and to put on the new self, created to be like God in true righteousness and holiness.

Notice how in those verses, Paul distinguishes how the Church is to be separated from the rest of the non-believing world (Gentiles). Paul would later write about the actions that are to differentiate the Church from Gentiles, but here we see his manner of separation is in thinking: "…you must no longer walk as the Gentiles do, in the futility of their thinking," and as translated in the New Living Translation (NLT), "Live no longer as the Gentiles do, for they are hopelessly confused." In the next sentence Paul clarifies what the source of this wrong thinking is: "They [Gentiles] are darkened in their understanding and alienated from the life of God because of the ignorance that is in them due to the hardness of their hearts." Those who do not believe in Christ are obscured in their understanding and are separated from God due to their ignorance. If you are a born-again believer of the one true God who sent His son Jesus to bear our sins, there is available divine revelation for how to live life as God intended it. However, if you deny God, deny Jesus, deny the Holy Spirit, then life is lived as though in a thick mist: truth being obscured and only ever viewed in part. Notice the word "ignorance," Paul is describing the dark situation unbelievers are in due to a lack of knowledge. Paul, however, does not stop at ignorance and instead explains that this ignorance is due to "hardness of heart."

Paul in his letter to the Romans can give us a bit more insight to this "hardness of heart" in Romans 1:18-23 in the New American Standard Bible (NASB):

> For the wrath of God is revealed from heaven against all ungodliness and unrighteousness of people who suppress the truth in unrighteousness, because

that which is known about God is evident within them; for God made it evident to them. For since the creation of the world His invisible *attributes, that is,* His eternal power and divine nature, have been clearly perceived, being understood by what has been made, so that they are without excuse. For even though they knew God, they did not honor Him as God or give thanks, but they became futile in their reasonings, and their senseless hearts were darkened. Claiming to be wise, they became fools, and they exchanged the glory of the incorruptible God for an image in the form of corruptible mankind, of birds, four-footed animals, and crawling creatures.

The Holy Spirit gives revelation that this is not a description of a people who do not know God, rather that this is a people who "did not honor Him as God or give thanks, but they became futile in their reasonings," a people who claimed to be wise and instead set up idols in the form of that which was created and "corruptible." There are those who at one time accepted Jesus as their LORD but presently have ignored His reasonings and His Word for their own reasoning and ideas. In Ephesians 4:19, Paul would add that those who have hardened hearts have "lost all sense of shame" for they have "given themselves over to sensuality for the practice of every kind of impurity, with a craving for more." In this current age, sensuality has a sexual connotation. Paul here simply means "sense-driven" which goes beyond just the sexual but as deriving pleasure from the senses and putting that before what God holds as important (not allowing ourselves to be so consumed with doing what "feels good"). Contrast that with what Paul writes to the church in Colossae (Colossians 3:1-3, BSB): "Therefore, since you have been raised with Christ, strive for the things above, where Christ is seated at the right hand of God. Set your minds on things above, not on earthly things. For you died, and your life is now hidden with Christ in God." The Holy Spirit through the epistles is urging us to set our hearts and minds on that which is above, our LORD Jesus Christ, not the sensual world here around us.

Looking back at Ephesians 4:22-24, Paul gives a reminder about what we are to do in keeping ourselves separated from the world: "... put off your former way of life, your old self, which is being corrupted by its deceitful desires; to be renewed in the spirit of your minds; and to put on the new self, created to be like God in true righteousness and holiness." Separate yourself from your old desires and instead renew the spirit of your mind. What does renewing your mind look like? Back to Romans in the BSB, though this time Romans 12:1-3:

> Therefore I urge you, brothers, on account of God's mercy, to offer your bodies as living sacrifices, holy and pleasing to God, which is your spiritual service of worship. Do not be conformed to this world, but be transformed by the renewing

> of your mind. Then you will be able to test and approve what is the good, pleasing, and perfect will of God.
>
> For by the grace given me I say to every one of you: Do not think of yourself more highly than you ought, but think of yourself with sober judgment, according to the measure of faith God has given you.

Utilizing our faith in God, the faith He gave us, we are to apply sober judgment to ourselves. We must stop and reflect upon our actions, our thinking, and our intentions. By inviting God to examine our hearts and minds through the Holy Spirit, we can discover those places where we have faltered and we can repent in that moment, making a change in our thinking and our actions through a conscious decision. This is living in the Will of God. This is glorifying God in word and in deed. This is a witness to the nations that will bring notice to who God is. We will discuss more in later chapters about our appropriate response to God, but the very first step is turning to Him. The Word is rich with many examples of those who turn their attention to God, repenting of a mindset or a belief in the heart, even if there was not a sinful action. We are to endeavor to learn more of the goodness of God, allowing His righteousness, not our own, be our saving grace. We must repent both of our sins and our dead works in that neither will bring us closer to God. Take time today and invite the LORD into your heart to examine it. Consider the following prayer and let it aid you as you practice repentance:

> LORD God in Heaven, how great is Your mercy and goodness! I thank You for sending Jesus of Nazareth down to earth to be the one time sacrifice for my sins. I invite you to work in me through Your Holy Spirit. Examine my thoughts and my mind, search out the deepest places of my heart. Help me to see where I have missed You or have fallen off the straight path you have laid before me. Show me where in my life unforgiveness is holding me back so that I may forgive others and myself for no other reason than to bring glory to Your Name. I am no longer the old creature but a new creation in Christ. I make a no turning back decision to be led by You and Your Spirit from this day forward. I soften my heart to You and humbly seek to serve you in a deeper way today. It is in the Name of the LORD Jesus Christ, I pray, Amen.

Repentance in the form of turning our heart and mind to God is a first step in the walk of faith. Take that step today towards God and let Him lead you in His mercy and grace. The next step is to know what His grace and His mercy mean for us as believers in the scope of our covenant.

What is Covenant?

Chapter 6 - First Mention of Favor/Grace in the New Testament

> In the sixth month, God sent the angel Gabriel to a town in Galilee called Nazareth, to a virgin pledged in marriage to a man named Joseph, who was of the house of David. And the virgin's name was Mary. The angel appeared to her and said, "Greetings, you who are **highly favored**! The Lord is with you."
>
> Mary was greatly troubled at his words and wondered what kind of greeting this might be. So the angel told her, "Do not be afraid, Mary, for you have found **favor** with God. Behold, you will conceive and give birth to a son, and you are to give Him the Name Jesus. He will be great and will be called the Son of the Most High. The Lord God will give Him the throne of His father David, and He will reign over the house of Jacob forever. His kingdom will never end!"
>
> - Luke 1:26-33, Berean Standard Bible (BSB)

To begin this section, we will start by examining the favor of God. We will examine some places in Scripture where God pours out His favor on a chosen people, a people He has made a covenant with. Favor and covenant are deeply connected.

The initial appearance of "highly favored" comes from a derivation of the word we will study in depth, 'charis'. Verse 28 can be read as, "Hail, full of grace, the Lord is with thee: blessed art thou among women," in the Douay-Rheims Translation (DRB). So we see here that Mary is chosen by God to bear His son, Jesus. In this way, Mary is to go from just another law-abiding Jew to become the mother of the King. Mary is not from the line of David, the kingly lineage from where the messiah is expected to come, yet, through the intervention of God, she would have a place in history as someone who would receive great honor and glory for the son she would bear. Why her though? What qualified her as worthy? Let us compare two responses to the herald of God.

We will examine both the response of Mary to being told she will have a baby as well as the response of Zechariah, a relative of Mary, to his being told he will have a baby. We read in Luke 1:38 (BSB), ' "I am the Lord's servant," Mary answered. "May it happen to me according to your word." Then the angel left her. ' Notice here that Mary submits fully to the Will of the Father despite the fact that never in recorded history has a virgin become pregnant without being intimate with a man. She asks the means in which it would happen but she does not doubt the Word of God as given by this angel. The second response to Gabriel we want to investigate actually comes before in verse 18. When Gabriel tells a faithful man of God, Zechariah, that he and his wife will bear a son, Luke 1:18 gives us these words, ' "How can I be sure of this?" Zechariah asked the angel. "I am an old man, and my wife is well along in years." ' The LORD had done exactly this same miracle for

Abraham, an act that as a priest, Zechariah would know very well. However, Zechariah began to doubt based on his situation and because of it, he would be made mute until the day John, his son, is born. All of this helps us to understand why some are favored: believing the Word of the LORD, in the life of the Jew, resulted in the outpouring of God's favor. [Notice that Zechariah receives a miracle but the word 'favor' is not used in verse 1-23, though Elizabeth will proclaim in verse 25 that the LORD has shown her favor after this sign of making Zechariah mute]. Let us dig more into what 'favor' and 'grace' mean and how they apply to us who are not Jews.

The word translated 'favor' above in the verses from Luke above is the same word translated 'grace' in much of the New Testament, the word *'charis.'* From the HELPS Word-studies, we have the following definitions:

> Cognate: 5485 *xáris* (another feminine noun from *xar-*, "*favor, disposed to, inclined, favorable* towards, *leaning towards* to share benefit") – properly, *grace*. 5485 (*xáris*) is preeminently used of the Lord's *favor* – freely *extended to give Himself away* to people (because He is "always leaning toward them").

> 5485 /*xáris* ("grace") answers directly to the Hebrew (OT) term 2580 /*Kaná* ("grace, *extension-toward*"). Both refer to God *freely extending* Himself (*His favor*, grace), *reaching* (*inclining*) to people because He is *disposed* to bless (be near) them.

> [5485 (*xáris*) is sometimes rendered "thanks" but the core-idea is "*favor, grace*" ("*extension towards*").]

There is this idea of extending something to another person; blessing an individual with something. A powerful example of the word *'charis'* appears in Luke 6 after Jesus tells His disciples to love their enemies. Luke 6:32-36 (BSB) reads:

> If you love those who love you, what **credit** is that to you? Even sinners love those who love them. If you do good to those who do good to you, what **credit** is that to you? Even sinners do the same. And if you lend to those from whom you expect repayment, what **credit** is that to you? Even sinners lend to sinners, expecting to be repaid in full.

> But love your enemies, do good to them, and lend to them, expecting nothing in return. Then your reward will be great, and you will be sons of the Most High; for He is kind to the ungrateful and wicked. Be merciful, just as your Father is merciful.

The word above translated 'credit' is that same word for 'grace.' We see here that grace acts as a settling of 3 different accounts: when love is shown, when good is done, and when debts are paid. Moreover, Jesus contrasts each of these by saying how His followers are to live and act differently by not looking for that credit. So favor and grace then must be an extension of a blessing not to those to whom it is owed, rather to those who are not worthy! This indicates that favor and grace truly are not earned, nor should they be expected as a response for our actions.

The word *'charis'* appears 157 times in the New Testament. It is seen in Luke, John, Acts, Romans, 1 Corinthians, 2 Corinthians, Galatians, Ephesians, Philippians, Colossians, 1 Thessalonians, 2 Thessalonians, 1 Timothy, 2 Timothy, Titus, Philemon, Hebrews, James, 1 Peter, 2 Peter, 2 John, Jude, and Revelation. That's 5-6 distinct authors who wrote the majority of the books of the New Testament! This ought to stamp for us the importance of the favor and grace of God in our lives. Before we dig more into the New Testament usage of grace/favor, let us look at the first usage in the Old Testament (one-for-one translations given in the Greek translation of the Old Testament, the Septuagint) of the word *'kana,'* that Hebrew transliteration of *'charis.'*

In the second chapter of this book, we investigated the 6th chapter of Genesis with regards to the early days of man and the part Noah had to play. In Genesis 6, verses 5-7, God talks about the evil in man and how it grieved Him to see man in such a state. Genesis 6:8 then reads, 'Noah, however, found **favor** in the eyes of the LORD.' The first usage of the word *'kana'* is in regards to Noah and is contrasted by the actions of other men at the time. In fact, verses 9, 11-13, 17-18, 22 (BSB) read as follows:

> This is the account of Noah. Noah was a righteous man, blameless in his generation; Noah walked with God...
>
> Now the earth was corrupt in the sight of God, and full of violence. And God looked upon the earth and saw that it was corrupt; for all living creatures on the earth had corrupted their ways. Then God said to Noah, "The end of all living creatures has come before Me, because through them the earth is full of violence. Now behold, I will destroy both them and the earth...
>
> And behold, I will bring floodwaters upon the earth to destroy every creature under the heavens that has the breath of life. Everything on the earth will perish. But I will establish My covenant with you, and you will enter the ark—you and your sons and your wife and your sons' wives with you..."
>
> So Noah did everything precisely as God had commanded him.

We see that Noah was righteous and that he walked with God. When he was given direction from God, he did precisely what was instructed of him. We can contrast this with the violent and corrupt nature of every other man on the face of the earth. Because of this difference, God extended His favor through grace and established a covenant with Noah. This covenant, established on Noah fulfilling the desire of the LORD by building and filling the ark, would lead to a promise that the LORD would not only bless Noah and his family, but all who come in their lineage by promising there would never again be destruction of all of the world by flood. This early interaction with covenant and its corresponding favor needs to be studied further for us to truly grasp what favor and grace mean. We will pick up our investigation of favor and grace in the next chapter after we uncover what a covenant is and what it means to have one.

Chapter 7 - Covenants of Promise

The first mention of covenant is in Genesis 6 (see the previous chapter of this book). More clarity on the meaning of a covenant comes in Genesis chapters 8 and 9, after the flood waters recede (Genesis 8:20-22, 9:1-17, BSB):

> Then Noah built an altar to the LORD. And taking from every kind of clean animal and clean bird, he offered burnt offerings on the altar. When the LORD smelled the pleasing aroma, He said in His heart, "Never again will I curse the ground because of man, even though every inclination of his heart is evil from his youth. And never again will I destroy all living creatures as I have done.
>
> As long as the earth endures,
> seedtime and harvest,
> cold and heat,
> summer and winter,
> day and night
> shall never cease."
>
> And God blessed Noah and his sons and said to them, "Be fruitful and multiply and fill the earth. The fear and dread of you will fall on every living creature on the earth, every bird of the air, every creature that crawls on the ground, and all the fish of the sea. They are delivered into your hand. Everything that lives and moves will be food for you; just as I gave you the green plants, I now give you all things. But you must not eat meat with its lifeblood still in it. And surely I will require the life of any man or beast by whose hand your lifeblood is shed. I will demand an accounting from anyone who takes the life of his fellow man:
>
> Whoever sheds the blood of man,
> by man his blood will be shed;
> for in His own image
> God has made mankind.
> But as for you,
> be fruitful and multiply;
> spread out across the earth
> and multiply upon it."
>
> Then God said to Noah and his sons with him, "Behold, I now establish My **covenant** with you and your descendants after you, and with every living creature that was with you—the birds, the livestock, and every beast of the earth—every

living thing that came out of the ark. And I establish My **covenant** with you: Never again will all life be cut off by the waters of a flood; never again will there be a flood to destroy the earth."

And God said, "This is the sign of the **covenant** I am making between Me and you and every living creature with you, a covenant for all generations to come: I have set My rainbow in the clouds, and it will be a sign of the **covenant** between Me and the earth.

Whenever I form clouds over the earth and the rainbow appears in the clouds, I will remember My **covenant** between Me and you and every living creature of every kind. Never again will the waters become a flood to destroy all life. And whenever the rainbow appears in the clouds, I will see it and remember the everlasting **covenant** between God and every living creature of every kind that is on the earth."

So God said to Noah, "This is the sign of the **covenant** that I have established between Me and every creature on the earth."

There is a lot here to unpack for us to truly understand what a 'covenant' is and the part it has to play in the favor and grace of God. The word used here for covenant is the Hebrew בְּרִית or 'berith' which Strong's Exhaustive Concordance defines as, 'confederacy, confederate, covenant, league. From barah (in the sense of cutting (like bara')); a compact (because made by passing between pieces of flesh) -- confederacy, (con-)feder(-ate), covenant, league.' Indicative of the importance of the word 'berith,' it is used in one form or another in 284 places across 28 books of the Old Testament. In fact, the word 'Testament' is a synonym for the word 'Covenant' and some translations actually distinguish the bible through the 'Old Covenant' and the 'New Covenant.' A further discussion on wills and testaments can be found later in chapter 8. We will examine covenants through a purely biblical lens, though I highly recommend E. W. Kenyon's book *The Blood Covenant* to strengthen your understanding of how covenants existed in the world outside of Israel and how it allowed ministers to bring the gospel to the heart of Africa when no one else could. Westerners do not view legal transactions in the same way that eastern cultures do. In the West, we live in a society where people seek to escape obligations and exploit loopholes. In many ways, this has led to a lack of trust between people because you can not take a person at their word. Not so with the people of Israel: when covenant was cut, the terms outlined in the covenant would be followed out exactly or severe curses follow [see Deuteronomy 28, 29, and 30 for blessings and curses under the Abrahamic Covenant as Moses was commanded to have the people declare].

Looking at the covenant Noah makes with God, the first thing that Noah does after exiting the ark with the animals and his family is offer up a sacrifice to the LORD, spilling blood and burning an offering to the LORD. Strong covenants are built upon blood as is indicated by the word itself, which implies the act of cutting being involved. This covenant comes with a sign and a blessing: a rainbow in the sky as a reminder that Noah and his descendants would be fruitful and multiply without fear of all of humanity being destroyed again by flood. The verse that we should really meditate on is verse 17 where God says, "This is the sign of the covenant that I have established between Me and every creature on the earth." Through the act of one man, the earth is blessed. The favor of God is exhibited in this, an extension of blessing not just to those who perform an act (Noah), but to all who are included in the covenant. That is the grace of God in action!

Why is a covenant needed? What happened that God needed to seek an individual to carry out His will? One of the results of the above covenant with Noah is blessings coming unto mankind. We see this also in the beginning, as we read in Genesis, God creating man on the sixth day and blessing him (Genesis 1:27-31, BSB):

> So God created man in His own image;
> in the image of God He created him;
> male and female He created them.
>
> God blessed them and said to them, "Be fruitful and multiply, and fill the earth and subdue it; rule over the fish of the sea and the birds of the air and every creature that crawls upon the earth."
>
> Then God said, "Behold, I have given you every seed-bearing plant on the face of all the earth, and every tree whose fruit contains seed. They will be yours for food. And to every beast of the earth and every bird of the air and every creature that crawls upon the earth—everything that has the breath of life in it—I have given every green plant for food." And it was so.
>
> And God looked upon all that He had made, and indeed, it was very good.

We can compare the phrase, "breath of life" with what we read in Genesis 2:7 (BSB), 'Then the LORD God formed man from the dust of the ground and breathed the breath of life into his nostrils, and the man became a living being.[d]' The footnote reads '7 d Or *a living soul*; cited in 1 Corinthians 15:45' which helps us to better understand the statement that man was created in the "image of God." God is a spirit. As a spirit, He moves through space and time and He set the universe in motion at creation (consider Genesis 1:2 (BSB), 'Now the earth was formless and void, and darkness was over the surface of the deep.

And the Spirit of God was hovering over the surface of the waters.') Man was first crafted through physical means, molded from the dirt. Man, however, is not fully alive until God breathes life into him. Since God is not a physical being but is a spiritual being, the implication is that this breath is not purely air but also the impartation of spirit. So God creates man and then fills him with spirit. Assuming nothing changes, man would continue to live in the blessings that the LORD imparted to him at creation.

Genesis 2:17 in the Literal Standard Version (LSV) gives a condition to this life in the Garden of Eden, "...but from the Tree of the Knowledge of Good and Evil, you do not eat from it, for in the day of your eating from it—dying you die." Most translations give the last part as "certainly you will die" but in the Hebrew "certainly" does not appear. Instead the word for death appears in two different forms. This should not be overlooked (since there was never a condition for physical death prior to it) and indicates two deaths: a physical death (the body's separation from its spirit and soul) and a spiritual death (the separation of our spirit from God's Spirit). We see that in eating of the fruit of the Tree of Knowledge of Good and Evil, the man and woman bring about a spiritual death that separates them from God, allowing physical death to happen. Man had a relationship and deep fellowship with God, but this one sin broke both the fellowship and relationship with God. Ever since, God has desired for this relationship to be repaired. Covenant is how God recreates that bond. Grace makes it such that, in the eyes of God, sin never happened. The covenant with Noah was just the beginning of God bringing His beloved creation back into relationship with Him.

Another covenant of particular interest is the covenant that Abraham has with the LORD God. In fact, this covenant is the most notable covenant and is what is referred to as the Abrahamic covenant. For what reason would God create a covenant with Abraham? First, let us go to Genesis 12:1-5 (BSB), before Abram became Abraham. [It is important to note that "Abram" and "Abraham" are the same person and the name used in Scripture will indicate whether it was before or after God changes his name, similarly with "Sarai" and "Sarah"]:

> Then the LORD said to Abram, "Leave your country, your kindred, and your father's household, and go to the land I will show you.
>
> I will make you into a great nation,
> and I will bless you;
> I will make your name great,
> so that you will be a blessing.
> I will bless those who bless you
> and curse those who curse you;

> and all the families of the earth
> will be blessed through you."
>
> So Abram departed, as the LORD had directed him, and Lot went with him. Abram was seventy-five years old when he left Haran. And Abram took his wife Sarai, his nephew Lot, and all the possessions and people they had acquired in Haran, and set out for the land of Canaan.

Notice that Abram is 75 years old at this proclamation of a future blessing. Abram and Sarai, although in their 70s, had yet to bear any children. This blessing implied that they would have children, since "a great nation" requires more than two people. Years go by and battles are fought in the following chapters of Genesis until chapter 15 where Abram is showing his concern that he will die before seeing the promise fulfilled. Genesis 15:2-6 (BSB) reads as:

> But Abram replied, "O Lord GOD, what can You give me, since I remain childless, and the heir of my house is Eliezer of Damascus?" Abram continued, "Behold, You have given me no offspring, so a servant in my household will be my heir."
>
> Then the word of the LORD came to Abram, saying, "This one will not be your heir, but one who comes from your own body will be your heir." And the LORD took him outside and said, "Now look to the heavens and count the stars, if you are able." Then He told him, "So shall your offspring be."
>
> Abram believed the LORD, and it was credited to him as righteousness.

The LORD stirs confidence in Abram, confirming His original promise to Abram. Because Abram believed, we see that "it was credited to him as righteousness," it is always valuable to believe what the LORD says! The LORD even gives a vivid visual example for Abram with the uncountable number of stars in the sky. Yet, Abram waivers by taking matters into his own hands 11 years later (Genesis 16:1-2,15-16, BSB):

> Now Abram's wife Sarai had borne him no children, but she had an Egyptian maidservant named Hagar. So Sarai said to Abram, "Look now, the LORD has prevented me from bearing children. Please go to my maidservant; perhaps I can build a family by her."
>
> And Abram listened to the voice of Sarai…
>
> And Hagar bore Abram a son, and Abram gave the name Ishmael to the son she had borne. Abram was eighty-six years old when Hagar bore Ishmael to him.

The LORD continues to bless Abram and Sarai, though the birth of Ishmael through Sarai's servant brings strife for the family (Genesis 16:12, BSB, tells us that, "He will be a wild donkey of a man, and his hand will be against everyone, and everyone's hand against him; he will live in hostility toward all his brothers.") Then, 24 years after giving the original promise, the LORD appears to Abram again (Genesis 17:1-8, BSB):

> When Abram was ninety-nine years old, the LORD appeared to him and said, "I am God Almighty. Walk before Me and be blameless. I will establish My covenant between Me and you, and I will multiply you exceedingly."
>
> Then Abram fell facedown, and God said to him, "As for Me, this is My covenant with you: You will be the father of many nations. **No longer will you be called Abram, but your name will be Abraham**, for I have made you a father of many nations.
>
> I will make you exceedingly fruitful; I will make nations of you, and kings will descend from you.
>
> I will establish My covenant as an everlasting covenant between Me and you and your descendants after you, to be your God and the God of your descendants after you.
>
> And to you and your descendants I will give the land where you are residing—all the land of Canaan—as an eternal possession; and I will be their God."

Notice, at 75, Abram was given a promise. At 99, Abram is offered a covenant. The promise had to come before the covenant so that Abram could be prepared for what was to be asked of him. Abram had to practice his faith all of those years to be ready for this moment. The LORD then gives specifics of the covenant: 1) all males party to the covenant are to be circumcised (remember that a covenant required cutting of some kind), both born of the family and purchased slaves, and 2) the line will come through Sarai (name changed to Sarah). Notice also a covenant name change, the LORD would put part of His name (the H, or "hey" from YHWH, which can be read as "yod-hey-vav-hey" though it was also known as the "unspeakable name of God" to the Jews so they would not likely read it aloud, the representation of 'LORD' in the Old Testament) in both Abram and Sarai so they would become AbraHam and SaraH. Compare that to the modern-day example of changing or hyphenating a last name in marriage. Marriage is meant to be a form of covenant that would join two people to be closer than blood relatives. In fact, many aspects of marriage come from early covenant ceremonies: the bringing and exchanging of gifts; the binding together as seen in some cultures and in centuries past, there would even be a cutting of both bride and groom so their blood would be mingled; a sacrifice of an animal and accompanying feast; the changing of one or both names; an officiant of the agreement who would oversee the vows promised to each other. Over millennia since covenant was first created and introduced to man and woman, the marriage rite has devolved and with it, the collective belief in the power and importance of marriage as the unifying not only of two people but of two families, bound to an agreement made on behalf of the bride and groom. With that context, let us turn our attention back to Abraham.

Twenty-five years after first appearing to Abram, the covenant is cut and the way for the promise to be fulfilled has become manifest! Let us review that promise from chapter 11 again, "I will make you into a great nation, and I will bless you; I will make your name great, so that you will be a blessing. I will bless those who bless you and curse those who curse you; and **all the families of the earth** will be blessed through you." Abram persevered for 25 years to become Abraham and to finally have a son born to him after cutting a covenant with the Almighty God, but notice the phrase above that is bolded for emphasis. The blessings that would come on Abraham through the covenant would also come on the families of the earth, not just those of the lineage of Isaac, Abraham's son through Sarah. Paul digs into this further in his letter to the Galatian church, (Galatians 3:6-9):

> So also, "Abraham believed God, and it was credited to him as righteousness." Understand, then, that those who have faith are sons of Abraham. The Scripture foresaw that God would justify the Gentiles by faith, and foretold the gospel to Abraham: "All nations will be blessed through you." So those who have faith are blessed along with Abraham, the man of faith.

Notice that phrase "the Scripture foresaw." A blessing guaranteed to Abraham for his faith would come to those of us who were not a part of that same covenant because God knew a new covenant would have to come. A covenant that, like Abraham's, would require a life of faith. The interconnectedness of Scripture is so powerful and reveals so much to us the nature and power of God!

Chapter 8 - Uncircumcised Philistine

In the first chapter we discussed Saul as the first king of Israel. Before his fall, Saul and Israel often clashed with a group of people called the Philistines. The Philistines predated the Israelites in Canaan and were said to be a massive people. In Joshua 13:1-7 (BSB), Joshua talks about taking land from the Philistines as it was part of the promise from God to Abraham:

> Now Joshua was old and well along in years, and the LORD said to him, "You are old and well along in years, but very much of the land remains to be possessed. This is the land that remains:
>
> All the territory of the Philistines and the Geshurites, from the Shihor east of Egypt to the territory of Ekron on the north (considered to be Canaanite territory)—that of the five Philistine rulers of Gaza, Ashdod, Ashkelon, Gath, and Ekron, as well as that of the Avvites; to the south, all the land of the Canaanites, from Mearah of the Sidonians to Aphek, as far as the border of the Amorites; the land of the Gebalites; and all Lebanon to the east, from Baal-gad below Mount Hermon to Lebo-hamath.
>
> All the inhabitants of the hill country from Lebanon to Misrephoth-maim—all the Sidonians—I Myself will drive out before the Israelites. Be sure to divide it by lot as an inheritance to Israel, as I have commanded you. Now therefore divide this land as an inheritance to the nine tribes and the half-tribe of Manasseh."

Joshua, who brings the Israelites into the land promised them by God after Moses brings them out of Egypt, indicates that there is quite a bit of work to be done. Part of that work is defeating the Philistines. Any Israelite who knew the Abrahamic Covenant would know that this was their rightful inheritance. The book of Joshua is full of the successful conquests of the Israelite people because they knew what was promised them and they acted on it. It did not require extensive religious teaching to grasp, just the firm belief that the Word of God is true.

David, even as a boy, was one such person who acted on the promises of God as though they were true. David carried with him a boldness that contrasted his physical frame, a young boy of ruddy complexion who tended to the sheep. We are told, however, in 1 Samuel 16 that the LORD chooses David to be anointed as king by Samuel after the LORD removes the anointing from Saul. This anointing does not change things much for David. David knows about his covenant with the Most High God and that is what gives him a boldness unlike anyone else. One day when he is bringing food to his brothers on the battlefield, David sees a giant, Goliath, that is causing the army of Israel to cower. David's response is given in 1 Samuel 17:26 (BSB),

> David asked the men who were standing with him, "What will be done for the man who kills this Philistine and removes this disgrace from Israel? Just who is this **uncircumcised** Philistine, that he should defy the armies of the living God?"

David did not fear the giant simply on the basis of circumcision. What does circumcision have to do with courage and power? Remember that circumcision was the mark the LORD required of Abraham for all who would be party to the covenant with God. David knew that he was in covenant with God and Goliath was not. Moreover, David would know that this land was part of their inheritance meaning that the Philistines had to go. The boldness of David is shown as he goes to King Saul in 1 Samuel 17:34-37 (BSB),

> David replied, "Your servant has been tending his father's sheep, and whenever a lion or a bear came and carried off a lamb from the flock, I went after it, struck it down, and delivered the lamb from its mouth. If it reared up against me, I would grab it by its fur, strike it down, and kill it. Your servant has killed lions and bears; this uncircumcised Philistine will be like one of them, for he has defied the armies of the living God." David added, "The LORD, who delivered me from the claws of the lion and the bear, **will deliver me** from the hand of this Philistine."

David had seen the promises of God in action. He had a confident assurance that he would succeed. He had exercised his faith and had come out victorious because he had confidence in whom he believed. In the face of Goliath, an impossible circumstance, David chose to believe God over the fear of failure that everyone else around him embraced. David had his mind right (recall our conversation on repentance in the first section of this book) by keeping the promises of God in his heart and choosing to focus on them rather than the situations in front of him that would take out anyone who did not have God to carry them through.

Recall that we have discussed both Abraham and David and the massive struggles that they overcame. How were they able to do it? They stood on what God said. They knew what God had said about their situation, how God had already planned for success, and they both chose to believe what God said. Noah had to be obedient to what the LORD told Him despite how it sounded. Can you imagine building a massive boat in the middle of the desert? Noah could and Noah did. Can you imagine having children well past your 70s? Abram could- such that he became Abraham. Can you imagine, as a youth, going up against a literal giant who terrified an entire army? David could and David did. To see how we are affected in this day and age, let us shift our focus to Jesus!

Chapter 9 - Seeing Jesus in the Covenant

The terms of Abraham's covenant were such that his offspring would be privy to the same covenant. But how would it come to pass that the rest of the nations would be blessed? What would take place that would present the opportunity that someone not born of Abraham would receive a blessing? Throughout the Old Testament there are allusions to a Messiah, a savior of the Jewish people. There are many prophecies of one who would bear the sins of the people, prophecies like Isaiah 53:12, (BSB): "Therefore I will allot Him a portion with the great, and He will divide the spoils with the strong, because He has poured out His life unto death, and He was numbered with the transgressors. Yet He bore the sin of many and made intercession for the transgressors." In the Jewish Law, there were certain offerings that were made unto God on behalf of the sins of the people. Yet in this prophecy, it could be seen that a person was to be sacrificed. There are prophecies of one who would save the people, like in Jeremiah 23:5,6 (BSB): "Behold, the days are coming, declares the LORD, when I will raise up for David a righteous Branch, and He will reign wisely as King and will administer justice and righteousness in the land. In His days Judah will be saved, and Israel will dwell securely. And this is His name by which He will be called: The LORD Our Righteousness." There are also verses like Joel 2:32 that says (BSB), "And everyone who calls on the name of the LORD will be saved..." There are verses like Genesis 49:10; Numbers 24:17,19; Psalm 60:7; Psalm 2:7-9; Isaiah 42:1,4 and many others that led the Jewish people to be on the lookout for a coming Messiah. To those who were looking and waiting for the Messiah, they saw the fulfillment of the Scriptures in Jesus: His being a descendant of David through Joseph, the virgin birth, being born in Bethlehem yet being known from Nazareth. Miracle after miracle being done in the midst of the people, teaching about what the heart of the Word of God is and not just the letter of the Law. The horrible torture and disfigurement of Jesus and His sacrifice on the cross. His burial, descent into "Hades" and then His resurrection after three days to be seen in the streets before going into Heaven to be seated at the right Hand of the Father. There was much in the Scriptures that would point people to be actively waiting for a Messiah and to receive Jesus as that Messiah, one who would bring a blessing to all people.

During the time of Jesus' ministry (and even now), there are those that question the divinity of Jesus. Verse after verse in the Old Testament point to who the Messiah would be, where He would come from, and what He would do. Paul preaches about Jesus and how He is that foretold Messiah, making connections using Scripture throughout the Old Testament to make the case for Christ. Acts 13:16-41 (BSB) reads as follows:

> Paul stood up, motioned with his hand, and began to speak: "Men of Israel and you Gentiles who fear God, listen to me! The God of the people of Israel chose our fathers. He made them into a great people during their stay in Egypt, and with an

uplifted arm He led them out of that land. He endured their conduct for about forty years in the wilderness. And having vanquished seven nations in Canaan, He gave their land to His people as an inheritance. All this took about 450 years.

After this, God gave them judges until the time of Samuel the prophet. Then the people asked for a king, and God gave them forty years under Saul son of Kish, from the tribe of Benjamin. After removing Saul, He raised up David as their king and testified about him: 'I have found David son of Jesse a man after My own heart; he will carry out My will in its entirety.'

From the descendants of this man, God has brought to Israel the Savior Jesus, as He promised. Before the arrival of Jesus, John preached a baptism of repentance to all the people of Israel. As John was completing his course, he said, 'Who do you suppose I am? I am not that One. But He is coming after me whose sandals I am not worthy to untie.'

Brothers, children of Abraham, and you Gentiles who fear God, it is to us that this message of salvation has been sent. The people of Jerusalem and their rulers did not recognize Jesus, yet in condemning Him they fulfilled the words of the prophets that are read every Sabbath. And though they found no ground for a death sentence, they asked Pilate to have Him executed.

When they had carried out all that was written about Him, they took Him down from the tree and laid Him in a tomb. But God raised Him from the dead, and for many days He was seen by those who had accompanied Him from Galilee to Jerusalem. They are now His witnesses to our people.

And now we proclaim to you the good news: What God promised our fathers He has fulfilled for us, their children, by raising up Jesus. As it is written in the second Psalm:

'You are My Son;
today I have become Your Father.'

In fact, God raised Him from the dead, never to see decay. As He has said:

'I will give you the holy and sure blessings promised to David.'

So also, He says in another Psalm:

'You will not let Your Holy One see decay.'

> For when David had served God's purpose in his own generation, he fell asleep. His body was buried with his fathers and saw decay. But the One whom God raised from the dead did not see decay.
>
> Therefore let it be known to you, brothers, that through Jesus the forgiveness of sins is proclaimed to you. Through Him everyone who believes is justified from everything you could not be justified from by the law of Moses. Watch out, then, that what was spoken by the prophets does not happen to you:
>
> 'Look, you scoffers,
> wonder and perish!
> For I am doing a work in your days
> that you would never believe,
> even if someone told you.'"

There are many to whom Paul preached (as well as those to whom Jesus preached) that scoffed at the message of the forgiveness of sins by one Jesus Christ. Though there were also many who recognized Jesus for who He was, the true Messiah from the line of David. This can be seen in the way that some who needed healing called out to Him.

Matthew's account of the Gospel makes some of the most compelling arguments for Jesus being the Christ [note: 'Christ' is the Greek for 'Messiah' or 'Anointed One']. We see three examples in Matthew of people calling out to Jesus as the "Son of David," revealing that each of them had the revelation that Jesus was the fulfillment of the Scriptures as their Messiah. Starting with Matthew 9:27-30 (BSB), we are given an account of Jesus healing two blind men:

> As Jesus went on from there, two blind men followed Him, crying out, "Have mercy on us, Son of David!"
>
> After Jesus had entered the house, the blind men came to Him. "Do you believe that I am able to do this?" He asked.
>
> "Yes, Lord," they answered.
>
> Then He touched their eyes and said, "According to your faith will it be done to you." And their eyes were opened. Jesus warned them sternly, "See that no one finds out about this!"

The phrase "have mercy" comes from covenant. Oftentimes in a covenant, there is a difference in power or ability between the two joined parties. Requesting mercy speaks to an acknowledgment of the power that the greater possesses and requests that they would bless or protect the lesser. Though the New Testament was written in the Greek, the Hebrew word for 'mercy' that the Jews of the region would know is חֶסֶד or 'checed,' also translated as goodness or loving-kindness. Throughout the Old Testament, it can be seen that the people of God would implore Him to show 'checed' to them, not because they deserve it, but because the very nature of God is to be good and to be merciful. Read through Psalms and look for the words 'mercy' or 'loving-kindness' to see just how prevalent the use of it is. The covenant that God had with the Israelites granted them protection and mercy. Just as David did, many Jews throughout the Old Testament did as these two blind men did and called on the mercy of God that is promised them through covenant. What we read in Matthew 15:21-28 (BSB) shows something a bit different in that a non-Jew is calling out to Jesus in the same way that the Jews who are party to the covenant would:

> Leaving that place, Jesus withdrew to the district of Tyre and Sidon. And a Canaanite woman from that region came to Him, crying out, "Lord, Son of David, have mercy on me! My daughter is miserably possessed by a demon."
>
> But Jesus did not answer a word. So His disciples came and urged Him, "Send her away, for she keeps crying out after us."
>
> He answered, "I was sent only to the lost sheep of the house of Israel."
>
> The woman came and knelt before Him. "Lord, help me!" she said.
>
> But Jesus replied, "It is not right to take the children's bread and toss it to the dogs."
>
> "Yes, Lord," she said, "even the dogs eat the crumbs that fall from their master's table."
>
> "O woman," Jesus answered, "your faith is great! Let it be done for you as you desire." And her daughter was healed from that very hour.

This woman who is not from the line of Abraham, Isaac, and Jacob, a woman who does not have a covenant with God, is shown the 'checed' of God. Why? The secret to both this healing and that of the two blind men comes in Jesus' response: their faith has done the work. Read both sections of Scripture again and notice that the faith of the one desiring a miracle, not Jesus' faith, brought forth the miracle. This is further distinguished by the actions of Jesus: He laid His hands on the blind man but not on the daughter of the woman. In both cases, however, He spoke of their faith. As we read before in Galatians 3, the Scriptures (through Jesus) saw into the future, connecting true faith in a Word spoken by God to a guaranteed blessing. Compare this to how Abraham had built his faith by thinking on the promises of God or how David continually reminded himself of the covenant he had with the Almighty God. How good is it to know what we are promised and to stand on those promises! We are reminded again of that portion of the blessing of Abraham we bolded earlier: and all the families of the earth will be blessed through you [Abraham]. Abraham being faithful and doing his part opened up a blessing that would reach to all of mankind, a blessing this Canaanite woman experienced that day. This is a shadow of the covenant that would be forged in the blood of Jesus that would bring redemption to all people (more on that later).

The last example from this book is from Matthew 20:29-34 (BSB) with two more blind men as Jesus is leaving Jericho:

> As they were leaving Jericho, a large crowd followed Him. And there were two blind men sitting beside the road. When they heard that Jesus was passing by, they cried out, "Lord, Son of David, have mercy on us!"
>
> The crowd admonished them to be silent, but they cried out all the louder, "Lord, Son of David, have mercy on us!"
>
> Jesus stopped and called them. "What do you want Me to do for you?" He asked.
>
> "Lord," they answered, "let our eyes be opened."
>
> Moved with compassion, Jesus touched their eyes, and at once they received their sight and followed Him.

The *'checed'* of God through Jesus is seen by the use of the word 'compassion' here. The LORD, moved with compassion, spares these men from blindness. These men had to invoke the covenant they knew they had. More than that, they had to overcome the loud crowd admonishing them. Let this be a reminder to us that as we follow Jesus that we do not admonish those who desperately need Jesus but instead live our lives demonstrating the *'checed'* of God.

Chapter 10 - A Better Covenant

What does a covenant between Abraham and God have to do with us? For those who are born Jewish, the blessings of Genesis 18 are very clear when the LORD God says, "I will establish My covenant as an everlasting covenant between Me and you and your descendants after you, to be your God and the God of your descendants after you. And to you and your descendants I will give the land where you are residing—all the land of Canaan—as an eternal possession; and I will be their God." The blessings of this covenant (note that the term 'Old Testament' can also be read 'Old Covenant') do not seem to connect with those who are not born of the line of Isaac. What does it mean for us? There is much spoken in Galatians and Ephesians about this comparison between covenants, but for now let us go to Hebrews 6:13-20; 7:1-3, 11-28 (BSB):

> When God made His promise to Abraham, since He had no one greater to swear by, He swore by Himself, saying, "I will surely bless you and multiply your descendants." And so Abraham, after waiting patiently, obtained the promise.
>
> Men swear by someone greater than themselves, and their oath serves as a confirmation to end all argument. So when God wanted to make the unchanging nature of His purpose very clear to the heirs of the promise, He guaranteed it with an oath. Thus by two unchangeable things in which it is impossible for God to lie, we who have fled to take hold of the hope set before us may be strongly encouraged.
>
> We have this hope as an anchor for the soul, firm and secure. It enters the inner sanctuary behind the curtain, where Jesus our forerunner has entered on our behalf. He has become a high priest forever in the order of Melchizedek.
>
> This Melchizedek was king of Salem and priest of God Most High. He met Abraham returning from the slaughter of the kings and blessed him, and Abraham apportioned to him a tenth of everything. First, his name means "king of righteousness." Then also, "king of Salem" means "king of peace." Without father or mother or genealogy, without beginning of days or end of life, like the Son of God, he remains a priest for all time.
>
> Now if perfection could have been attained through the Levitical priesthood (for on this basis the people received the law), why was there still need for another priest to appear—one in the order of Melchizedek and not in the order of Aaron? For when the priesthood is changed, the law must be changed as well.

He of whom these things are said belonged to a different tribe, from which no one has ever served at the altar. For it is clear that our Lord descended from Judah, a tribe as to which Moses said nothing about priests.

And this point is even more clear if another priest like Melchizedek appears, one who has become a priest not by a law of succession, but by the power of an indestructible life. For it is testified:

"You are a priest forever
in the order of Melchizedek."

So the former commandment is set aside because it was weak and useless (for the law made nothing perfect), and a better hope is introduced, by which we draw near to God.

And none of this happened without an oath. For others became priests without an oath, but Jesus became a priest with an oath by the One who said to Him:

"The Lord has sworn and will not change His mind:

'You are a priest forever.'"

Because of this oath, Jesus has become the guarantee of a better covenant.

Now there have been many other priests, since death prevented them from continuing in office. But because Jesus lives forever, He has a permanent priesthood. Therefore He is able to save completely those who draw near to God through Him, since He always lives to intercede for them.

Such a high priest truly befits us—One who is holy, innocent, undefiled, set apart from sinners, and exalted above the heavens. Unlike the other high priests, He does not need to offer daily sacrifices, first for His own sins and then for the sins of the people; He sacrificed for sin once for all when He offered up Himself. For the law appoints as high priests men who are weak; but the oath, which came after the law, appointed the Son, who has been made perfect forever.

The writer of Hebrews cites from both Genesis and Psalms as they point to Jesus as the "guarantee of a better covenant" by pointing to him as our High Priest. This message was meant to speak directly to Jews and show to them that the Messiah they were waiting for had indeed come in the form of Jesus, that He fulfills what the Law had set to do. The author of Hebrews here does three interesting things: 1) he identifies the importance of a guarantee where covenants/oaths are concerned, 2) he identifies why Jesus is our High

Priest even though Jesus was not of the line of priests (Levites), 3) he identifies a briefly mentioned character from Genesis as important and connected with Jesus in a meaningful way. There is much to be gained in terms of revelation by reading through Hebrews after spending any amount of time reading Genesis, Exodus, Leviticus, Numbers, or Deuteronomy (the five together are also called the Pentatuch). Hebrews 8:6-13 (BSB) quotes from the prophet Jeremiah in telling us the following:

> Now, however, Jesus has received a much more excellent ministry, just as the covenant He mediates is better and is founded on better promises. For if that first covenant had been without fault, no place would have been sought for a second. But God found fault with the people and said:
>
> "Behold, the days are coming, declares the Lord,
> when I will make a new covenant
> with the house of Israel
> and with the house of Judah.
> It will not be like the covenant
> I made with their fathers
> when I took them by the hand
> to lead them out of the land of Egypt,
> because they did not abide by My covenant,
> and I disregarded them,
>
> *declares the Lord.*
>
> For this is the covenant I will make
> with the house of Israel
> after those days,
> declares the Lord.
> I will put My laws in their minds
> and inscribe them on their hearts.
> And I will be their God,
> and they will be My people.
> No longer will each one teach his neighbor or his brother,
> saying, 'Know the Lord,'
> because they will all know Me,
> from the least of them to the greatest.
> For I will forgive their iniquities
> and will remember their sins no more."
>
> By speaking of a new covenant, He has made the first one obsolete; and what is obsolete and aging will soon disappear.

So as we have read, a covenant is cut between two parties and involves blessing in such a way that others are blessed. We have also read that through Jesus, a new covenant is cut and the old becomes replaced by it. In this new covenant, sins are not simply covered as they had been before but forgotten, for the LORD said that He would "remember their sins no more." Think about that for a moment before we continue: God says that He would no longer remember our sins when He forgives us. Let this be a defining measure of how forgiveness should work in our lives; forgiving of past hurts means no longer bringing them up. We must quit bringing up the hurts of the people we have forgiven but we must also quit reminding God (and ourselves) of our own former sins. If it is truly forgiven, leave it behind.

Notice also that He said "I will put My laws in their minds and inscribe them on their hearts." This points towards God giving His Spirit to indwell us, ever giving correction and guidance to the born-again believer. Jesus Himself mentions covenant during that last Passover meal with His disciples as seen in Matthew 26:26-28 (BSB):

> While they were eating, Jesus took bread, spoke a blessing and broke it, and gave it to the disciples, saying, "Take and eat; this is My body."
>
> Then He took the cup, gave thanks, and gave it to them, saying, "Drink from it, all of you. This is My blood of the covenant, which is poured out for many for the forgiveness of sins."

Likewise in Mark 14:22-24 (BSB):

> While they were eating, Jesus took bread, spoke a blessing and broke it, and gave it to the disciples, saying, "Take it; this is My body."
>
> Then He took the cup, gave thanks, and gave it to them, and they all drank from it. He said to them, "This is My blood of the covenant, which is poured out for many."

As well as Luke 22:19-20 (BSB):

> And He took the bread, gave thanks and broke it, and gave it to them, saying, "This is My body, given for you; do this in remembrance of Me."
>
> In the same way, after supper He took the cup, saying, "This cup is the new covenant in My blood, which is poured out for you."

Notice that the meal that Jesus and His disciples were having was in remembrance of when the Angel came over Egypt killing every firstborn son except where there was the blood of the lamb over the doorpost as God instructed the Israelites. This is a foreshadowing of the Blood of the Lamb in the form of Jesus to protect those who partake in the meal with Him. Who is called to this meal? In the sixth chapter of John, Jesus is recorded as feeding five thousand people with a few loaves of bread. There are some who were so enamored with Jesus' teaching that day and the miracle in multiplying the bread, they followed Jesus a long way to inquire of Him the signs He worked. Jesus will connect His miracles with the coming covenant meal in John 6:26-65 (BSB):

> Jesus replied, "Truly, truly, I tell you, it is not because you saw these signs that you are looking for Me, but because you ate the loaves and had your fill. Do not work for food that perishes, but for food that endures to eternal life, which the Son of Man will give you. For on Him God the Father has placed His seal of approval."
>
> Then they inquired, "What must we do to perform the works of God?"
>
> Jesus replied, "The work of God is this: to believe in the One He has sent."
>
> So they asked Him, "What sign then will You perform, so that we may see it and believe You? What will You do? Our fathers ate the manna in the wilderness, as it is written: 'He gave them bread from heaven to eat.' "
>
> Jesus said to them, "Truly, truly, I tell you, it was not Moses who gave you the bread from heaven, but it is My Father who gives you the true bread from heaven. For the bread of God is He who comes down from heaven and gives life to the world."
>
> "Sir," they said, "give us this bread at all times."
>
> Jesus answered, "I am the bread of life. Whoever comes to Me will never hunger, and whoever believes in Me will never thirst. But as I stated, you have seen Me and still you do not believe.
>
> Everyone the Father gives Me will come to Me, and the one who comes to Me I will never drive away. For I have come down from heaven, not to do My own will, but to do the will of Him who sent Me.
>
> And this is the will of Him who sent Me, that I shall lose none of those He has given Me, but raise them up at the last day. For it is My Father's will that everyone who looks to the Son and believes in Him shall have eternal life, and I will raise him up at the last day."
>
> At this, the Jews began to grumble about Jesus because He had said, "I am the bread that came down from heaven." They were asking, "Is this not Jesus, the son

of Joseph, whose father and mother we know? How then can He say, 'I have come down from heaven?'"

"Stop grumbling among yourselves," Jesus replied. "No one can come to Me unless the Father who sent Me draws him, and I will raise him up at the last day. It is written in the Prophets: 'And they will all be taught by God.' Everyone who has heard the Father and learned from Him comes to Me— not that anyone has seen the Father except the One who is from God; only He has seen the Father.

Truly, truly, I tell you, he who believes has eternal life. I am the bread of life. Your fathers ate the manna in the wilderness, yet they died. This is the bread that comes down from heaven, so that anyone may eat of it and not die. I am the living bread that came down from heaven. If anyone eats of this bread, he will live forever. And this bread, which I will give for the life of the world, is My flesh."

At this, the Jews began to argue among themselves, "How can this man give us His flesh to eat?"

So Jesus said to them, "Truly, truly, I tell you, unless you eat the flesh and drink the blood of the Son of Man, you have no life in you. Whoever eats My flesh and drinks My blood has eternal life, and I will raise him up at the last day. For My flesh is real food, and My blood is real drink.

Whoever eats My flesh and drinks My blood remains in Me, and I in him. Just as the living Father sent Me and I live because of the Father, so also the one who feeds on Me will live because of Me. This is the bread that came down from heaven. Unlike your fathers, who ate the manna and died, the one who eats this bread will live forever."

Jesus said this while teaching in the synagogue in Capernaum. On hearing it, many of His disciples said, "This is a difficult teaching. Who can accept it?"

Aware that His disciples were grumbling about this teaching, Jesus asked them, "Does this offend you? Then what will happen if you see the Son of Man ascend to where He was before?

The Spirit gives life; the flesh profits nothing. The words I have spoken to you are spirit and they are life. However, there are some of you who do not believe." (For Jesus had known from the beginning which of them did not believe and who would betray Him.)

> Then Jesus said, "This is why I told you that no one can come to Me unless the Father has granted it to him."

Jesus' disciples that struggled with this message would understand if only they would heed what Jesus said, "the Spirit gives life; the flesh profits nothing." Jesus is not talking in the physical but in the spiritual. This is not a message of cannibalism but a message that prioritizes the spiritual food of fellowship with Father God through Jesus Christ. The Jewish people had a relationship with the LORD God because of their covenant but not all of them actively pursued fellowship with Him. Jesus offers the relationship with the Father through Him as the sacrificial lamb. As the High Priest seated at the right hand of God, Jesus also offers us fellowship with the Father that would otherwise be impossible. Jesus opened the way with a new covenant with God. This covenant becomes open to anyone who would believe in Jesus and profess Him as Lord. The above verses reveal those who followed the ministry of Jesus, saw His many miracles, heard His bold teaching, but still would not make space in their hearts for Him to be their Lord.

Jesus spoke about offering His Body and Blood in that sixth chapter of John. We also know that blood is an important part of any covenant. Hebrews chapter nine gives a great contrast between the Abrahamic Covenant and the New Covenant in Jesus, in particular verses 13-15 (BSB) showing a comparison in blood:

> For if the blood of goats and bulls and the ashes of a heifer sprinkled on those who are ceremonially unclean sanctify them so that their bodies are clean, how much more will the blood of Christ, who through the eternal Spirit offered Himself unblemished to God, purify our consciences from works of death, so that we may serve the living God!

> Therefore Christ is the mediator of a new covenant, so that those who are called may receive the promised eternal inheritance, now that He has died to redeem them from the transgressions committed under the first covenant.

The Holy Spirit through the author of Hebrews illuminates the purpose of the Blood of Christ in this New Covenant and why it is important: blood is a part of the purification rite because "the life of a creature is in the blood, and I [God] have given it to you to make atonement for yourselves on the altar; it is the blood that makes atonement for one's life," Leviticus 17:11 (BSB). The Abrahamic Covenant would have required yearly sacrifices but Hebrews 9:25-28 (BSB) reminds us that this not so with Christ:

> Nor did He enter heaven to offer Himself again and again, as the high priest enters the Most Holy Place every year with blood that is not his own. Otherwise, Christ would have had to suffer repeatedly since the foundation of the world. But now He

has appeared once for all at the end of the ages to do away with sin by the sacrifice of Himself.

Just as man is appointed to die once, and after that to face judgment, so also Christ was offered once to bear the sins of many; and He will appear a second time, not to bear sin, but to bring salvation to those who eagerly await Him.

We see some contrasts here between the covenants: the blood of animals covers or makes atonement for one's sins whereas the Blood of Jesus washes away sin, remitting it so that it was like sin never happened. Sacrifices are made continually in the Old Covenant so that man may again fellowship with God but the one time sacrifice of Jesus on the cross permits us continual fellowship with the Father that we could never deserve. Forgiveness in the Old Covenant required bringing our sacrifice to the altar so a high priest could make an offering to God. Forgiveness in the New Covenant requires us going to God through Jesus and acknowledging what Jesus did on the cross for us as our High Priest. The Old Covenant was hindered by what we were capable of doing since we are not able to fulfill the Law. The New Covenant is perfected by what Jesus did for us, removing the need for a merit-based system since it is Jesus who has done the work.

Compare "covenant" back to the word "testament," often used in the context of "last will and testament." A person's will and testament pertains to what is guaranteed to an individual or organization after the passing of someone. In this transaction, the person who receives from this transaction does not have to do anything to receive. There is not a qualification; the person is deceased and then they cede their personal belongings to another party. In the same way, Jesus died and we are guaranteed into the covenant He cut. Read through the Gospels (Matthew, Mark, Luke, and John) and see for yourself where Jesus tells of His coming sacrifice and how it would mark a new era, an era that we are called to be a part of. An era of genuine relationship with the Father God. An era in which we can fellowship with Him as easily as we fellowship with anyone in the physical realm.

If you have accepted Jesus as your LORD, renew your mind to the eternal covenant you have with Him. Call upon His Name in faith as the blind men did and receive healing. The Name of Jesus is yours, use it with the same boldness as His disciples. Receive His *'checed'* in your life and allow His favor to fill your life. Know that you have a covenant with the Most High God. If you do not know God, invite Him into your life. The covenant is as easy to join as confessing "Jesus is LORD" with your mouth and believing it in your heart. Just as miracles were wrought in calling out to Jesus to have mercy prior to His death, miracles to include your salvation are wrought in His resurrection. Affirm your covenant with the Almighty God with this prayer:

Father God in Heaven, how great is Your Name! You sent Jesus down with a most holy Name so that I would be redeemed from death and destruction. How merciful is my LORD! How worthy He is to be praised! I say thank you for Jesus and I ask that you reveal to my spirit a greater knowledge of Your covenant with me for I have a covenant with the Most High God. Show me all of Your mercies. Show me all of Your goodness. By faith I take my healing, it is my right. By faith I take restoration of finances, it is my right. I am forgiven not because I am worthy but because you are good. The Blood of Jesus, my LORD, purifies me so that I may better serve my God. All glory and honor is Yours, Almighty Father, forever and ever. It is in the Name of Your Son, Jesus I pray. Amen.

There are many more verses that cover the blessings of our covenant. We will endeavor to tackle a few of them in the next chapter but take time now to meditate on what you've read. An unrepentant heart will not truly understand covenant. Without knowing your legal right through covenant, what good is it to talk about what it guarantees? Allow the LORD to speak to you through what you have read so that you may receive from Him according to His desires for you. The LORD has the prophet Jeremiah (29:11-4a, BSB) deliver a message to the people that is as much a message for you as it is for them:

> For I know the plans I have for you, declares the LORD, plans to prosper you and not to harm you, to give you a future and a hope. Then you will call upon Me and come and pray to Me, and I will listen to you. You will seek Me and find Me when you search for Me with all your heart. I will be found by you, declares the LORD…

What is Grace?

Chapter 11 - Defining Grace with Mercy and Peace

> God did not reject His people, whom He foreknew. Do you not know what the Scripture says about Elijah, how he appealed to God against Israel: "Lord, they have killed Your prophets and torn down Your altars. I am the only one left, and they are seeking my life as well"?
>
> And what was the divine reply to him? "I have reserved for Myself seven thousand men who have not bowed the knee to Baal."
>
> In the same way, at the present time there is a remnant chosen by **grace**. And if it is by **grace**, then it is no longer by works. Otherwise, **grace** would no longer be **grace**.
>
> - Romans 11:2-6, Berean Standard Bible (BSB)

In the last chapter, we saw that the first mention of '*charis*' is in context with how the favor of God was upon Mary. One could think it was because of her piety or how she lived her life. In his letter to the Romans, Paul, as guided by the Holy Spirit, helps us to define '*charis*' more richly. In the above verses, Paul quotes Elijah as he appeals to the LORD in his time of need. We are reminded of the covenant '*checed*' that Elijah had, the mercy that would protect Elijah in dire circumstances. With the invocation of the LORD's mercy, Paul identifies that God's response is one of grace, or '*charis*.' The LORD had chosen Elijah, but He had chosen others as well. Of His chosen ones, there were seven thousand and one who "have not bowed the knee to Baal," a local deity of the region that the Israelites often found themselves submitting to. Paul reminds the reader that the remnant was chosen by '*charis*' and says that at that time, in Paul's time, God had chosen a remnant. The next sentence is of particular interest to us as we define '*charis*,' '...if it is by grace, then it is no longer by works.' So then we must ask ourselves: was Mary chosen to be favored by God because of her good conduct? The answer must be no. Instead, Mary is chosen due to lineage. Go back to Matthew 1:1-17 and Luke 3:23-38 and see the emphasis on bloodlines and order of progression, both for Joseph and for Mary.

Throughout his writings, Paul speaks of grace and peace from the Father as an impartation to whom he writes. The words used are '*charis*' for grace and '*eirene*' for peace. '*Eirene*,' as we will study, is used as the transliteration of the Hebrew word '*shalom*.' '*Shalom*' is a word that is translated as 'peace' but the meaning is much greater than that. As defined by HELPS Word-Study, *eirēnē* (from *eirō*, "to *join, tie together* into *a whole*") – properly, *wholeness*, i.e. when all essential parts are joined together; *peace* (God's gift of *wholeness*). Compare this to '*shalom*', which defined by Strong's Exhaustive Concordance can be taken to mean well, favor, friend, great, good health, perfect; Or *shalom* {shaw-lome'}; from shalam; safe, i.e. (figuratively) well, happy, friendly; also (abstractly) welfare, i.e. Health, prosperity, peace -- X do, familiar, X fare, favour, + friend, X great, (good) health, (X perfect, such as be at) peace(-able, -ably), prosper(-ity, -ous), rest, safe(-ty), salute, welfare, (X all is, be) well, X wholly. We see that the implication is to have wholeness and welfare. Now that we have a stronger understanding of the words, let us see them in use. The bolding is added for emphasis of the words '*charis*' and '*eirene*.'

2 Thessalonians 3:16 (Amplified Bible, AMP): "Now may the LORD of **peace** Himself grant you His **peace** at all times *and* in every way [that peace and spiritual well-being that comes to those who walk with Him, regardless of life's circumstances]. The Lord be with you all."

Ephesians 1:2 (Passion Translation, TPT): "... May God Himself, the Heavenly Father of our LORD Jesus Christ, release **grace** over you and impart **total well being** into your lives."

1 Corinthians 1:3 (TPT): "May joyous **grace*** and **endless peace** be yours continually from our Father God and from our LORD Jesus Christ, the Anointed One."

> Footnote: *1:3 The Greek word '*charis*,' in its original sense, is descriptive of that which brings pleasure and joy to the human heart, implying a strong emotional element. God's grace includes favor and supernatural potency and it is meant to leave us both charming and beautiful. In classical Greek it was meant to convey the attitude of favor by royalty.

Imagine walking along and you catch the eye of someone you know is wealthy. This person, who perhaps you know the name of but you do not know personally, calls you over and puts in your hand the keys to a brand new car. Did you do something to deserve this? Did you earn it? Is this the universe "leveling the playing field" as many philosophers would like to say? No, this is grace. This is a kind act bestowed onto someone else that produces elation. A kind act, notably, that is not earned (recall Romans 11:6 from above). It is the nature of God to give.

Consider also the condition of the heart in the act of giving. Cain and Abel both gave gifts to God. Genesis 4:2-5 (BSB) is given as the following: "...Now Abel was a keeper of sheep, while Cain was a tiller of the soil. So in the course of time, Cain brought some of the fruit of the soil as an offering to the LORD, while Abel brought the best portions of the firstborn of his flock. And the LORD looked with favor on Abel and his offering, but He had no regard for Cain and his offering. So Cain became very angry, and his countenance fell." Why did the LORD approve of Abel's offering but not Cain's? Abel gave the "best portions of the firstborn of his flock," Cain brought "some of the fruit." The argument to be made here is not that "God prefers meat to fruit" but that God desires the very best in a gift. Abel set out to give the best he had rather than to save it for himself. Cain gave out of obligation.

First Samuel shows us a case in which two priests (Hophni and Phineas) were performing immoral acts by taking from the meat offering to the LORD. Chapter 2 verse 17 (BSB) gives the clear charge against the men: "Thus the sin of these young men was severe in the sight of the LORD, for they were treating the LORD's offering with contempt." There was a heavy weight for their sin because of the way they treated the LORD's offering.

Jesus spoke to His disciples while at the temple about giving by the contrast of one widow woman to the many rich donors. Mark 12:41-44 and Luke 21:1-4 tell of Jesus sitting at the treasury watching people give their gifts to God (what criticism would He face doing that in this age!) and He observed a widow woman give. Levitical law would dictate that the church would take care of widows in the event they are not of the age to marry again. This woman was dependent on the church and donations from the church to live and have her needs met. Both Mark and Luke specifically state she is a "poor widow woman" with Luke quantifying that the amount of money given was equal to a small portion of the common Roman currency of the time. Despite this, Jesus states she gives more than anyone else. Mark 12:44 and Luke 21:4 (BSB) give the rationale, "For they all contributed out of their surplus, but she out of her poverty has put in all she had to live on." It's not the gift alone but the heart behind the gift. The woman comes forward with a posture of sacrifice, wholly reliant on God to meet her needs.

First Kings describes another widow who gave all she had and her needs were provided for beyond what she gave. The prophet Elijah is traveling during a time of famine and the Word of the LORD comes to him (1 Kings 17:8-14, BSB):

> Then the word of the LORD came to Elijah: "Get up and go to Zarephath of Sidon, and stay there. Behold, I have commanded a widow there to provide for you."
>
> So Elijah got up and went to Zarephath. When he arrived at the city gate, there was a widow gathering sticks. Elijah called to her and said, "Please bring me a little water in a cup, so that I may drink." And as she was going to get it, he called to her and said, "Please bring me a piece of bread."
>
> But she replied, "As surely as the LORD your God lives, I have no bread—only a handful of flour in a jar and a little oil in a jug. Look, I am gathering a couple of sticks to take home and prepare a meal for myself and my son, so that we may eat it and die."

"Do not be afraid," Elijah said to her. "Go and do as you have said. But first make me a small cake of bread from what you have, and bring it out to me. Afterward, make some for yourself and your son, for this is what the LORD, the God of Israel, says: 'The jar of flour will not be exhausted and the jug of oil will not run dry until the day the LORD sends rain upon the face of the earth.'"

Obeying what Elijah spoke to her, the woman was blessed beyond the meager amount she had. Giving with a willing heart, believing that God will provide, opened the widow woman up to receive from the LORD. In the same way, with a heart open to being completely dependent upon God, we open ourselves up to receive from His grace.

There are few verses from the Bible as prolific as John 3:16; verses that regardless of belief or denomination, people seem to have some knowledge of. In the KJV, it reads: "For God so loved the world, that He gave His only begotten Son, that whosoever believeth in Him should not perish, but have everlasting life." Notice that God gave to us His Son. We also see this in Romans 8:32 in the BSB: "He who did not spare His own Son but gave Him up for us all, how will He not also, along with Him, freely give us all things?" This was not an act of earning the favor of God; rather as a free gift, Jesus was given. Likewise, Paul reveals to us that God will freely give us all things (more on that later). Less well known is John 3:17, which, in the KJV, reads as, "For God sent not His Son into the world to condemn the world; but that the world through Him might be **saved**." This word "saved" is the Greek 'sozo' which is defined by the HELPS Word-studies as *sōzō* (from *sōs*, "safe, rescued") – properly, *deliver* out of danger and *into safety*; used principally of God *rescuing* believers *from* the penalty and power of sin – *and into His provisions* (*safety*). [4982 (*sōzō*) is the root of: 4990 /*sōtēr* ("Savior"), 4991 /*sōtēría* ("salvation") and the adjectival form, 4992 /*sōtērion* (what is "*saved*/rescued *from* destruction *and brought into divine safety*").] We see that the use of this word is to move from a state of brokenness into a state of wholeness, or '*eirene*' Combine this with what we read in the last chapter through the miracles listed in Matthew when people invoked the healing power of Jesus through '*checed*,' we get a beautiful picture of how God works in the world: the '*checed*' or mercy of God grants us the opportunity to turn to His '*charis*' or grace which brings with it '*sozo*' or repairing of brokenness so that we may live in the '*eirene*' or '*shalom*,' perfect peace and wholeness, that the LORD desires for us.

Let us go back to 1 Corinthians to see what the grace of God looks like. 1 Corinthians 1:4-5 (TPT):

> I am always thanking my God for you because He has given you such free and open access to His **grace** through your union with Jesus, the Messiah. In Him you have been made extravagantly rich in every way. You have been endowed with a

> wealth of inspired utterance and the riches that come from your intimate knowledge of Him.

The grace that the LORD imparts to us brings with it riches and the wealth of inspired utterance. The LORD even guides our speech through "inspired utterance" - how impressive is our God! To get more clarification of the "intimate knowledge of Him," let us go down to verse 8 and 9 (1 Corinthians 1:8-9, TPT):

> He will keep you steady and strong to the very end, making your character mature so that you will be found innocent on the day of our LORD Jesus Christ. God is forever faithful and can be trusted to do this in you, for He has invited you to co-share the life of His Son*, the Anointed One, our King!

> Footnote: *1:9 Or "a communion with His Son." That is, a co-participation (communion, fellowship) of the Son. The Aramaic can be translated, "You have been called to the (wedding) feast of His Son." We see a clear picture here that believers are called to share in the sonship of Jesus. By God's grace, we will share in the Son's standing and position before the Father. We are not only blameless but made holy by the co-sharing of the life of God's Son.

Notice what God is doing in us: He keeps us strong and steady and makes our character mature. In the last chapter we discussed the fellowship that the Israelites had with God granted to them by their covenant. Through Jesus, we are called to fellowship with God not as lesser beings but *as equal to Jesus*. Jesus grants us life as we could not otherwise know it. John 3:15-18 (TPT) reads as follows:

> "... so that those who truly believe in Him [Jesus] will not perish but be given eternal life. For this is how much God loved the world - He gave His one and only Son as a gift. So now everyone who believes in Him* will never perish but experience eternal life. So now there is no longer any condemnation for those who believe in Him, but the unbeliever already lives under condemnation because they do not believe in the name of God's beloved Son."

> Footnote: *3:16 Or "believe into Him." Salvation and regeneration must be by faith. True faith (Gr. *'pistis'*) has a number of components: acceptance, embracing something (someone) as truth, union with God and His Word, and an inner confidence that God alone is enough.

It is through believing in Jesus that we are separated from the world. This separation allows for our rescuing from condemnation that is present here and now. Notice that the natural state of things without Jesus is condemnation.

Chapter 12 - What is Afforded Man Through Grace?

How many theosophies or philosophies speak to the suffering of man? How many people profess that hardships are just a part of the human experience? Jesus came to remove condemnation, but what about the suffering? The author of Romans expounds upon what is afforded us through the grace of God in Romans 5:1-11 (BSB):

> Therefore, since we have been justified through faith, we have peace with God through our Lord Jesus Christ, through whom we have gained access by faith into this grace in which we stand. And we rejoice in the hope of the glory of God.

[Note: Faith in the grace Jesus gives us provides justification, peace, and joy in the hope of the glory of God.]

> Not only that, but we also rejoice in our sufferings, because we know that suffering produces perseverance; perseverance, character; and character, hope. And hope does not disappoint us, because God has poured out His love into our hearts through the Holy Spirit, whom He has given us.

[Note: Sufferings will not go away in our believing in Christ. The right response to suffering, however, does produce spiritual growth because we have the Comforter, the Holy Spirit, living on the inside of us. Suffering produces perseverance which in turn produces character which in turn produces hope which has with it expectancy for what is to come.]

> For at just the right time, while we were still powerless, Christ died for the ungodly. Very rarely will anyone die for a righteous man, though for a good man someone might possibly dare to die. But God proves His love for us in this: While we were still sinners, Christ died for us.

[Note: This aligns with the message that Jesus preaches about how we are not to live in the "action and reaction" sense that the world lives in because our Heavenly Father has shown us that the true demonstration of love is the kind without condition. See "What is repentance?" for more clarification.]

> Therefore, since we have now been justified by His blood, how much more shall we be saved from wrath through Him! For if, when we were enemies of God, we were reconciled to Him through the death of His Son, how much more, having been reconciled, shall we be saved through His life! Not only that, but we also rejoice in God through our Lord Jesus Christ, through whom we have now received reconciliation.

We are justified, saved from wrath, reconciled to God, but not taken from suffering. As long as we live in the world (i.e., not in Heaven) we are surrounded by trials and tribulation. We are saved from a final judgment that will befall those who do not accept Jesus as LORD. More than that though, salvation brings forth a new spirit. This new spirit allows for a new connection to God.

The relationship that man had with God in the garden is reforged. Suffering remains in the world but something new emerges: the fellowship that Adam had in the beginning is reconciled for us through Jesus Christ. The relationship as equals we discussed in 1 Corinthians is included throughout the epistles of the New Testament, including in Ephesians 2:5-6 (BSB):

> But God still loved us with such great love. He is so rich in compassion and mercy. Even when we were dead and doomed in our many sins, He united us into the very life of Christ and saved us by His wonderful grace! He raised us up with Christ the exalted One … of the heavenly realm, for we are now co-seated as one with Christ!

The grace of God pulls us from death to life in Christ! The next few verses (Ephesians 2:7-9, TPT), shows a deeper understanding of what is afforded us in the grace imparted to us:

> Throughout the coming ages, we will be the visible display of the infinite, limitless riches of grace and kindness, which was showered upon us in Jesus Christ. For it was only through this wonderful grace that we believed in Him. Nothing we did could ever earn this salvation, for it was the gracious gift from God that brought us to Christ! So no one will ever be able to boast, for salvation is never a reward for good works or human striving.

This is the great contrast between humanism and Christianity: salvation is not a reward for your good acts or your efforts. There are many religions and philosophies that agree on the importance of love (Islam and Hinduism, for instance), the need for forgiveness (highly valued in many African cultures), and the difficulties faced in going through life alone (consider collectivist societies like those found among many Native American tribes). A life without Jesus though, is not life at all in that life without Jesus is life without God. These Scriptures we have read did not declare that the grace of God was a gift through your giving to charity or your being kind. The grace and kindness of God are riches that are given as free gifts for believing in Christ Jesus.

The philosophy of Taoism speaks of "the way" or a right path. Jesus tells us in John 14:6 (BSB) that, "I am the way and the truth and the life. No one comes to the Father except through Me." There is a path to enlightenment (higher knowledge and revelation). There is a path to God (or The Divine, as some believe). To think that all religion and philosophy are paths to the same destination though is a thought in error if that path does not include Jesus. Jesus said He is THE way, not a way. Good works would not earn the path to God. Upholding the Law was not the path to God. The redemptive work wrought in Jesus is the ONLY way to be in relationship with the Almighty.

Through Jesus, we have a way to cope with the suffering that is in the world today as well as have a new relationship with God in the same way Adam had in the Garden. To examine further what power and authority are brought in the grace of God, we must examine the person that is the Christ, Jesus: how He spoke and by what power He acted while on the earth.

Chapter 13 - Power in the Name of Jesus

Grace, as a free gift, is best understood in the ministry of Jesus. As we have seen in Scripture, He went about doing good, healing all who were sick and preaching the Good News. To better understand the workings of this ministry, let us dig into a facet of the Christ that is unique to Him: His Name is Jesus.

In His letter to the church in Philippi, Paul is inspired to write about the Name of Jesus. Paul's revelation of the power of the Name both at this time and in the coming judgment is worthy of our pondering (Philippians 2:5-11, BSB):

> Let this mind be in you which was also in Christ Jesus:
>
> Who, existing in the form of God,
> did not consider equality with God
> something to be grasped,
> but emptied Himself,
> taking the form of a servant,
> being made in human likeness.
> And being found in appearance as a man,
> He humbled Himself
> and became obedient to death—
> even death on a cross.
>
> Therefore God exalted Him to the highest place
> and gave Him the name above all names,
> that at the name of Jesus every knee should bow,
> in heaven and on earth and under the earth,
> and every tongue confess that Jesus Christ is Lord,
> to the glory of God the Father.

God the Father gave Jesus His Name. Jesus did not earn His Name but it was conferred upon Him. A similar example is in the knighting of a person in English tradition. Through some act of valor or honorable service, the English crown grants the title of "Sir" to anyone who is knighted. This is the act of conferring a name. Other people outside of England acknowledge the title of knight. Note here that in Philippians, Paul writes about Jesus gaining "the name above all names." There is no honor higher than the Name of Jesus. There is power in the Name of Jesus because at that Name, every knee should bow in the three realms: in heaven, on the earth, and under the earth. What power! What authority! What else is afforded in the Name of Jesus Christ?

The Holy Spirit had Paul write two letters to the church in Thessaloniki. The second letter has some profound revelation of what judgment will look like at the end of this age when Jesus comes again in glory. Telling of His second coming, 2 Thessalonians 1:10-12 (AMP) says:

> ...When He comes to be glorified in His saints in that day [that is, glorified through the changed lives of those who have accepted Him as Savior and have been set apart for His purpose], and to be marveled at among all who have believed, because our testimony to you was believed *and* trusted [and confirmed in your lives].

> With this in view, we constantly pray for you, that our God will count you worthy of your calling [to faith] and with [His] power fulfill every desire for goodness, and complete [your] every work in faith, so that the name of our LORD Jesus will be glorified in you [by what you do], and you in Him, according to the [precious] grace of our God and the LORD Jesus Christ.

Paul prays for the church for three things: 1) God will count them worthy of their calling, 2) that through His power, God would supply their every desire for goodness, 3) that God would complete their every work in faith. Think on that third point for a moment: God would do the work that is started by us. This tells us that God will not start the work He has asked us to do. Nor does He expect us to do the work by our ability or authority. The grace of God and Jesus is how Paul has authority to ask such a prayer, a prayer that when fulfilled would glorify the Name of our LORD Jesus. Paul delivers an amazing revelation here about how our actions bring glory to the Name of Jesus.

What does a name mean? We live in a day and age where a person can easily change their own name. Consider Saul's name change to Paul as determined by others in the Church, or the change from Simon to Peter as given by Jesus. Each of these changes of name are given by others. Matthew 1:21 tells us that an angel of the LORD told Joseph to name Mary's son "Jesus." Throughout the Old Testament we see a great reverence for "the Name of the LORD," David even stating that the temple that Solomon would build would be a "house for Your (God's) Holy Name" (1 Chronicles 29:16, BSB). Why does Paul specify that our actions would glorify the "Name of our LORD Jesus?"

John's gospel account ends with the following verses (John 20:30-31, BSB),

> Jesus performed many other signs in the presence of His disciples, which are not written in this book. But these are written so that you may believe that Jesus is the Christ, the Son of God, and that by believing you may have life in His name.

John says we would have life "in His Name." Life was brought to us by the grace of God through Christ Jesus which means that the grace of God is IN the Name of Jesus. The last words spoken by Jesus in Mark 16:15-18 (BSB) are directions to His church and pertain to the Name:

> Go into all the world and preach the gospel to every creature. Whoever believes and is baptized will be saved, but whoever does not believe will be condemned. And these signs will accompany those who believe: **In My name** they will drive out demons; they will speak in new tongues; they will pick up snakes with their hands, and if they drink any deadly poison, it will not harm them; they will lay their hands on the sick, and they will be made well.

Jesus gives His Name as the source from which the disciples will be able to do these works. This is not the first time that Jesus sends His followers out to preach the Good News of salvation. In Luke 10, Jesus sends out 72 disciples, telling them in 10:8-9 (BSB), "If you enter a town and they welcome you, eat whatever is set before you. Heal the sick who are there and tell them, 'The kingdom of God is near you.'" When they return in verse 17, they are elated by what they could do in Jesus' Name. Jesus' response is important for us to consider as believers. Luke 10:17-20 (BSB) gives the following:

> The seventy-two returned with joy and said, "Lord, even the demons submit to us in Your name."

> So He told them, "I saw Satan fall like lightning from heaven. Behold, I have given you **authority** to tread on snakes and scorpions, and over all the power of the enemy. Nothing will harm you. Nevertheless, do not rejoice that the spirits submit to you, but rejoice that your names are written in heaven."

The disciples who worked these miracles in Jesus' Name were able to do so because of the authority in that Name. To make sense of it in the world we live in, consider the following analogy:

A man approaches you and says he would like to award you a cash reward for doing a job for him. The man is poor in appearance and speaks in an uneasy sort of way. He tells you his name and the company he represents but you do not recognize either.

A second man approaches you, and makes an offer similar to the first, though this man is in a well tailored suit. The man speaks with confidence. You immediately recognize both the company he represents and his name. In fact, you know him to be a person of importance with that company, a company you trust.

The question is this: who would you do the job for? The factors that lead you to the second one are the confidence and clear authority with which that man carries. In addition, he represents a company you trust and you know of the man himself. Demons know the Name of Jesus and they cower before it. Consider the man in the region of the Gerasenes who was plagued by the legion of demons: in the New Living Translation (NLT) of Mark 5:7 the demons cry, "Why are you interfering with me, Jesus, Son of the Most High God? In the Name of God, I beg you, don't torture me!" Earlier in Mark's gospel Jesus is in the synagogue when a man with an "unclean spirit" approaches Jesus (Mark 1:24, NLT) crying, "Why are you interfering with us, Jesus of Nazareth? Have you come to destroy us? I know who you are—the Holy One of God!"

Sickness knows the Name of Jesus and it backs down from it. When exercised from a place of authority, there is incredible power in the Name of Jesus! Look at what Jesus said in response to the 72, "Nevertheless, do not rejoice that the spirits submit to you, but rejoice that your names are written in heaven." Jesus wanted to direct the attention away from what the disciples could do and instead to what was worth celebrating: their deeds were seen by the Most High God and they would be rewarded for it in heaven! How amazing the Name of Jesus is when used with righteous motivation!

Peter demonstrates the power and authority of the Name of Jesus in the Acts of the Apostles (often referred to as the book of "Acts"), the third chapter. Acts 3:1-10 (BSB) gives the following illustration of the power of the Name:

> One afternoon Peter and John were going up to the temple at the hour of prayer, the ninth hour. And a man who was lame from birth was being carried to the temple gate called Beautiful, where he was put every day to beg from those entering the temple courts. When he saw Peter and John about to enter, he asked them for money.
>
> Peter looked directly at him, as did John. "Look at us!" said Peter. So the man gave them his attention, expecting to receive something from them. But Peter said, "Silver or gold I do not have, but what I have I give you: **In the name of Jesus Christ of Nazareth**, get up and walk!"
>
> Taking him by the right hand, Peter helped him up, and at once the man's feet and ankles were made strong. He sprang to his feet and began to walk. Then he went with them into the temple courts, walking and leaping and praising God.

> When all the people saw him walking and praising God, they recognized him as the man who used to sit begging at the Beautiful Gate of the temple, and they were filled with wonder and amazement at what had happened to him.

As we read through this, let us become aware of what has happened and what is happening. Notice that Peter and John were heading to prayer in the temple. This was a regular act, both at this time after the resurrection of Jesus and before when Jesus was still with them. These two men took this path daily for much of their life. At the gate sat a crippled man. This man did not suffer an accident in his adult life that crippled him. This man had been crippled since birth. One could assume that the man had been begging here at this gate of the temple for a long time, perhaps years. This means that there is a strong likelihood that this man had seen Peter and John before, likely with Jesus. Remembering that the role Judas played in the ministry of Jesus was treasurer, we could assume that as they passed, this group gave alms to the beggar every time they came through. Now, much of this is guesswork and reading between the lines. What is not guesswork is that this crippled man "expected to receive something from them." This is not the same as 'hoping' to receive something. This man was fully ready to receive from these men and he was not disappointed! Peter used the Name of Jesus to bring healing to this man who had been unable to walk from birth! The response that Peter has is remarkable in its humility and his ability to give the glory to God (Acts 3:12-20, BSB):

> And when Peter saw this, he addressed the people: "Men of Israel, why are you surprised by this? Why do you stare at us as if by our own power or godliness we had made this man walk?

> The God of Abraham, Isaac, and Jacob, the God of our fathers, has glorified His servant Jesus. You handed Him over and rejected Him before Pilate, even though he had decided to release Him. You rejected the Holy and Righteous One and asked that a murderer be released to you. You killed the Author of life, but God raised Him from the dead, and we are witnesses of the fact.

> By faith in the Name of Jesus, this man whom you see and know has been made strong. **It is Jesus' Name and the faith that comes through Him** that has given him this complete healing in your presence.

> And now, brothers, I know that you acted in ignorance, as did your leaders. But in this way God has fulfilled what He foretold through all the prophets, saying that His Christ would suffer. Repent, then, and turn back, so that your sins may be wiped away, that times of refreshing may come from the presence of the Lord, and that He may send Jesus, the Christ, who has been appointed for you.

Peter identifies that it is the Name of Jesus and faith in that Name that brought this miracle into being. More than that, Peter took this time to preach Jesus to the people with such boldness and authority that the high priest and others of the temple asked "By what power or what name did you do this?" Acts 4:8-12 (BSB) gives us the response from Peter:

> Then Peter, filled with the Holy Spirit, said to them, "Rulers and elders of the people! If we are being examined today about a kind service to a man who was lame, to determine how he was healed, then let this be known to all of you and to all the people of Israel: It is by the Name of Jesus Christ of Nazareth, whom you crucified but whom God raised from the dead, that this man stands before you healed. This Jesus is
>
> 'the stone you builders rejected,
> which has become the cornerstone.'
>
> Salvation exists in no one else, for there is no other name under heaven given to men by which we must be saved."

There is power in the Name of Jesus! There is salvation in the Name of Jesus! This name is the same name that conferred the grace of God to us. This name that enabled the disciples to cast out demons, cleanse lepers, and allow the crippled to walk and the blind to see is the same name through which we have salvation, that complete restoration of our bodies in the form of physical healing, restoration of finances in the form of debt cancellation, restoration of mind by the healing of ailments like depression or anxiety. Miracles happen in the Name of Jesus! How? Why? Two factors must be considered, the authority and the power in the Name.

Chapter 14 - Understanding Authority and Power

In the verses we have been reading about the Name of Jesus, we see the use of words like "authority" and "power" presented. For instance, the "authority" given the 72 disciples in Luke 10:19 or the "authority" conferred upon all of His disciples as Jesus greets them after His resurrection in Matthew 28:18 are the same word, "*exousia*." HELPS Word-studies give the definition of the word as 1849 *eksousía* (from 1537 /*ek*, "out from," which intensifies 1510 /*eimí*, "*to be*, *being* as a right or privilege") – authority, *conferred* power; *delegated empowerment* ("authorization"), operating in a *designated jurisdiction*. In the New Testament, 1849 /*eksousía* ("*delegated* power") refers to the *authority* God gives to His saints – *authorizing them to act to the extent* they are *guided by faith* (*His* revealed word).

This is the same word used by the centurion when he asked Jesus to come and heal his servant. Matthew 8:5-9 (BSB) give us the following:

> When Jesus had entered Capernaum, a centurion came and pleaded with Him, "Lord, my servant lies at home, paralyzed and in terrible agony."
>
> "I will go and heal him," Jesus replied.
>
> The centurion answered, "Lord, I am not worthy to have You come under my roof. But just say the word, and my servant will be healed. For I myself am a man under **authority**, with soldiers under me. I tell one to go, and he goes; and another to come, and he comes. I tell my servant to do something, and he does it."

Of all of the people to seek Jesus for healing, we are faced in this scenario with a Roman centurion. For starters, Romans were definitely NOT Jews: very few knew the customs of the Jews and most all of them were paganistic and worshiped their own gods. This man, however, knew something about Jesus. He knew that Jesus had something that he needed: the ability to perform miracles. The centurion knew this with such certainty that Jesus would make the following statements hearing the centurion's response (Matthew 8:10-13, BSB):

> When Jesus heard this, He marveled and said to those following Him, "Truly I tell you, I have not found anyone in Israel with such great faith. I say to you that many will come from the east and the west to share the banquet with Abraham, Isaac, and Jacob in the kingdom of heaven. But the sons of the kingdom will be thrown into the outer darkness, where there will be weeping and gnashing of teeth."

Then Jesus said to the centurion, "Go! As you have believed, so will it be done for you." And his servant was healed at that very hour.

This man who likely does not know the Most High God is being commended for his faith! Why? Because he saw and respected the **authority** of Jesus, not simply the act of healing. This centurion put the utmost confidence in what Jesus said and did such that his servant was healed at a distance in that very hour!

This act of healing at a distance by having faith in the authority of Jesus sets a legal precedent that we should heed: a man who was not expressly given authority by Jesus to perform miracles called for the healing of someone close to him and that healing happened through faith. There are people who will want to say, "Jesus performed miracles because he was God," or, "the disciples performed miracles because they were assigned to do that," or even, "miracles were for the time of the disciples but that time has passed away." This example in Matthew strongly challenges those assertions. It is through faith in Jesus and His divine authority that miracles were worked in His day and have been done in the time since then. Miracles are happening now for those who have a confident assurance in what they believe will happen by the authority of Jesus.

A word of caution: this is not a magic formula. One cannot simply say, "In the Name of Jesus, be healed," without truly believing that the Name brings with it power to perform the works which you ask. In the nineteenth chapter of Acts, we see just such an example when a "magic formula" is applied and it produces laughable results. After seeing Paul work many miracles in the Name of Jesus, a group of 7 brothers decided to give it a try. Their story and the results of their endeavors are recorded in Acts 19:13-20 (BSB):

> Now there were some itinerant Jewish exorcists who tried to invoke the name of the Lord Jesus over those with evil spirits. They would say, "I bind you by Jesus, whom Paul proclaims." Seven sons of Sceva, a Jewish chief priest, were doing this.
>
> Eventually, one of the evil spirits answered them, "Jesus I know, and I know about Paul, but who are you?" Then the man with the evil spirit jumped on them and overpowered them all. The attack was so violent that they ran out of the house naked and wounded.
>
> This became known to all the Jews and Greeks living in Ephesus, and fear came over all of them. So the name of the Lord Jesus was held in high honor. Many who had believed now came forward, confessing and disclosing their deeds. And a number of those who had practiced magic arts brought their books and burned them in front of everyone. When the value of the books was calculated, the total

came to fifty thousand drachmas. So the word of the Lord powerfully continued to spread and prevail.

Notice that these men were not proclaiming the Name of Jesus with authority, instead they stated, "I bind you by Jesus, whom Paul proclaims." There is no certainty or authority in their usage of the Name, not because there is no power in the Name itself but because these men did not have faith in the Name. The story does not stop there. Even though these men did not have a relationship with Jesus and thereby lacked the authority to use the Name of Jesus, they brought glory and honor to that Name! People in turn held the Name in "high honor" and turned from witchcraft and paganism. How amazing that a single foible could result in this massive turning from witchcraft and destruction of magical texts! The footnote in the Berean Standard Bible gives a drachma as equivalent to a day's wage. The current federally mandated minimum wage is $7.25 (in 2022). A typical day of work in the US is considered 8 hours. This means that a "day's wages" for an American would be $58 dollars. Multiply that by fifty thousand and the value is $2,900,000 USD. The average hardcover book, according to Scribe Media, is about $26. This means that we can estimate that there were over one hundred thousand books on magic that were burned in front of everyone. There are many assumptions in these calculations that one could argue against but the fact remains that this incident was a powerful witness to the people to repent from magic and turn to the one true God.

As we have been looking at the usage of the power of the Name of Jesus, we have stumbled on the importance of faith in the Name. What is faith? What can we learn from Jesus in the usage of our faith?

Chapter 15 - Have the God Kind of Faith

In the first half of the 1900s, there was revival happening in the US. A large number of tent meetings and the like began happening with an incredible number of miraculous healings attributed to them. Some were hoaxes not unlike what we saw in Acts 19 with the seven sons of Sceva, but many were legitimate. This movement saw teaching from people like Oral Roberts, Kenneth E. Hagin, Kenneth Copeland as well as many others. These men taught from the Bible, teaching what was referred to as the "word of faith" message, a phrase coming from Romans 10:8. The context is best seen as Romans 10:4-10 (BSB):

> For Christ is the end of the law, to bring righteousness to everyone who believes.
>
> For concerning the righteousness that is by the law, Moses writes: "The man who does these things will live by them." But the righteousness that is by faith says: "Do not say in your heart, 'Who will ascend into heaven?' (that is, to bring Christ down) or, 'Who will descend into the Abyss?' (that is, to bring Christ up from the dead)."
>
> But what does it say? "The word is near you; it is in your mouth and in your heart," that is, the **word of faith** we are proclaiming: that if you confess with your mouth, "Jesus is Lord," and believe in your heart that God raised Him from the dead, you will be saved. For with your heart you believe and are justified, and with your mouth you confess and are saved.

This "word of faith" message led to many people experiencing healing, divine revelation, and other supernatural experiences. Notice that this "word of faith" is two-fold: confession with the mouth that "Jesus is LORD," and believing in your heart that God our Father raised Him from the dead. The result of this is a person who is "saved," or *soteria* from the root *sozo.* When we looked at this word in an earlier chapter, we saw that it meant wholeness. This wholeness has been demonstrated time and time again in tent meetings, churches, houses and any place where people gather with faith in Jesus. Jesus teaches on the principles of faith after demonstrating that by word alone a fig tree could be cursed and brought to nought in a 24 hour period. Mark 11:22-25 (BSB) gives the following response from Jesus:

> "Have faith in God," Jesus said to them. "Truly I tell you that if anyone says to this mountain, 'Be lifted up and thrown into the sea,' and has no doubt in his heart but believes that it will happen, it will be done for him. Therefore I tell you, whatever you ask for in prayer, believe that you have received it, and it will be yours.
>
> And when you stand to pray, if you hold anything against another, forgive it, so that your Father in heaven will forgive your trespasses as well."

Notice again the connection between saying and believing: "...if anyone **says**... and has no doubt in his heart but **believes** that it will happen, it will be done for him." To believe, and truly believe as Jesus uses it, there is to be no doubt in your heart. Furthermore, in the next sentence, Jesus tells us that "whatever you ask for in prayer, believe that you **have received it**, and it will be yours." This is not just the absence of doubt, but the sureness of heart of having already received what has been asked. Jesus teaches on prayer in various places in Scripture (we will look into this more in-depth in "What is a Christian?") and often makes the connection back to forgiveness as He does here. Forgiveness is a clear demonstration of the grace of God at work in our lives.

Chapter 16 - The Forgiving Power of Grace

Starting with the twelfth chapter of Romans through the end of that book, Paul gives direction to the church on how to live and interact with one another. Through the Holy Spirit, Paul writes the following in Romans 12:14-21 (BSB):

> Bless those who persecute you. Bless and do not curse. Rejoice with those who rejoice; weep with those who weep. Live in harmony with one another. Do not be proud, but enjoy the company of the lowly. Do not be conceited.
>
> Do not repay anyone evil for evil. Carefully consider what is right in the eyes of everybody. If it is possible on your part, live at peace with everyone.
>
> Do not avenge yourselves, beloved, but leave room for God's wrath. For it is written: "Vengeance is Mine; I will repay, says the Lord."
>
> On the contrary,
>
> "If your enemy is hungry, feed him;
> if he is thirsty, give him a drink.
> For in so doing,
> you will heap burning coals on his head."
>
> Do not be overcome by evil, but overcome evil with good.

Paul's guidance to the church is the message Jesus came to deliver, love your brother. This love is not a *'phileo'* reciprocal love (love as others love you) but an *'agape'* unconditional love (love as God loves you). Forgiveness is one of the many ways in which we see this love and the grace of God in action. Grace has often been defined as the "unmerited favor of God," the extension of God's ability we could never deserve. Note that we are to take from that and live our lives in similar fashion by overcoming evil with good. Paul writes in Ephesians 2:4-5 (BSB), "But because of His great love for us, God, who is rich in mercy, made us alive with Christ even when we were dead in our trespasses. It is by grace you have been saved!" Grace, therefore, is that power, that force that allows us to live a life so very different from the people around us. A life that tells a story of God's goodness. Grace then is what takes a narrative of a downtrodden, lowly existence and adds the clause, "...but the LORD..." which then becomes a tale of success and victory.

Another beautiful example for what the grace of God does for us is found in Colossians 2:13-14 (TPT):

This "realm of death" describes our former state, for we were held in sin's grasp. But now, we've been resurrected out of that "realm of death" never to return, for we are forever alive and forgiven our sins! He canceled out every legal violation we had on our record and the old arrest warrant that stood to indict us. He erased it all - our sins, our stained soul - he deleted it all and they cannot be retrieved! Everything we once were in Adam has been placed onto His cross and nailed permanently there as a public display of cancellation.

Notice how Paul describes this forgiveness as canceling "out every legal violation we had on our record and the old arrest warrant that stood to indict us." Forgiveness cleanses the convicted wrongs and indictments of wrongdoing. This is a powerful image for us to apply to others as was applied to us. Grace in action can be seen not only as our forgiveness but God giving us the strength to forgive others. Note that this forgiveness is not surface-level. These sins that Jesus washed away are deleted "and they cannot be retrieved." How often do we pull up past hurts? How often do we pronounce, "I forgive you," only to remind the person later on of that same hurt? Let us learn from the example set by Jesus when we forgive: removal of sins, not the covering. For us to forgive as the Father does, we are to remember those hurts no more. This will require strength, the strength of God, in fact. Grace is the strength of God extended to you. If we have been given the power and authority to exercise demons and heal the sick, we surely have the power and authority to forgive others.

Our God is a good God. Grace is one such manifestation of His goodness. As we described earlier, the *'checed'* or mercy of God grants us the opportunity to turn to His *'charis'* or grace which brings with it *'sozo'* or repairing of brokenness so that we may live in the *'eirene'* or *'shalom,'* perfect peace and wholeness, that the LORD desires for us. In addition, we saw that the Name of Jesus and the Blood of Jesus are powerful weapons in defeating the devil and his demons for the one who believes in Jesus Christ as his Savior. We saw that as one who carries Christ with us, we carry His authority and His power because He sent us. We also remember the sacrificial act of Jesus dying for us and the forgiveness it brought us, a forgiveness we are to extend to others. In each of these, it should become apparent that God's grace is more than just the "unmerited favor" God gives to us. Our study here should make it clear to each of us that God has called us to live out His grace as His extension on the earth. We are not called to simply be forgiven, but to forgive. We are not called simply to be healed or loosed of demons, but to go out and heal and liberate those who are oppressed as Jesus did. We are not simply called to have a relationship with God, but to bring our fellow man and woman into that relationship. The grace of God should have an obvious effect on our lives, making us appear beautiful to the world around us. Our prayer then should be for us to be taught of God the best way we can demonstrate this grace to the world around us:

> Almighty Father, how gracious are You! You have freely given me a life I could never deserve through Jesus, Your Son. I thank You for calling me to You and I accept this calling. Today, I endeavor to not back down from the darkness in this present world but to present the Light that is Jesus to it. May my life be a story that tells of your goodness and mercy. LORD, guide me today so that I may forgive those that hurt me, even myself. Show me now where unforgiveness is in my heart so that I may forgive and turn back to You. Guide me so that I would let the love You have shown me radiate out from me to this hurting world. Father, I say "yes" to the work You have called me to. I speak the Name of Jesus over hurting situations because I believe that the same power that saved me and brought me to wholeness will bring wholeness to others. I pray '*shalom*,' nothing missing, nothing broken, over this nation and the people in it. In the coming days, show me more of You and Your grace in action so that in turn I may share it with the world! In the Mighty Name of Jesus I pray, amen.

The grace of God affords us an unaffordable life because of the one-time sacrifice of Jesus. As we go about our day, let us make time to honor Him and remember what He has done, is doing, and will do in us, for us, and through us. This life is not a solo sport, we are to live in this deep relationship with the Father and share it with the world. In our next two sections we will investigate the appropriate reaction of a born-again Christian by first studying "What is a Christian?" and then addressing what our actions should be in "What Now?" Before you move into these next two sections, read back through the verses we have discussed. Build for yourself confident assurance of what God desires for you. Read Deuteronomy 28:1-14 so that you may see the promised blessings that the LORD had Moses deliver to the people. Those of us who believe in Jesus have a covenant that supersedes the first so these blessings are ours as well (review "What is a Covenant?"). Meditate on these and know that the LORD desires for you to increase. Meditate on the manifold grace of God!

What is a Christian?

Chapter 17 - Defining the term "Christian"

> Meanwhile those scattered by the persecution that began with Stephen traveled as far as Phoenicia, Cyprus, and Antioch, speaking the message only to Jews. But some of them, men from Cyprus and Cyrene, went to Antioch and began speaking to the Greeks as well, proclaiming the good news about the Lord Jesus. The hand of the Lord was with them, and a great number of people believed and turned to the Lord.
>
> When news of this reached the ears of the church in Jerusalem, they sent Barnabas to Antioch. When he arrived and saw the grace of God, he rejoiced and encouraged them all to abide in the Lord with all their hearts. Barnabas was a good man, full of the Holy Spirit and faith, and a great number of people were brought to the Lord.
>
> Then Barnabas went to Tarsus to look for Saul, and when he found him, he brought him back to Antioch. So for a full year they met together with the church and taught large numbers of people. The disciples were first called **Christians** at Antioch.
>
> - Acts 11:19-26, BSB

The word for Christian, simply enough, comes from the Greek word for Christ. *'Christianos'* or Χριστιανός is given here in Antioch, a city which is in modern-day Turkey. The term is not from fellow believers but rather Gentiles. Let us use this bit of Scripture to define the term. We see that initially the disciples were, "speaking the message only to Jews," but later on some of them, "went to Antioch and began speaking to the Greeks as well." So we see that a Christian and disciple of Christ will speak the message of Jesus to both the Jews and the non-Jews (in this case, Greek). In preaching this message, a great number believed and, "turned to the LORD." We see that Barnabas lives as an example to Christians by rejoicing and encouraging his fellow believers to, "abide in the LORD with all of their hearts." Finally, in the twenty-sixth verse, we see that they, "met together with the church and taught large numbers of people." This is to be an example for us that a Christian should meet together with other Christians and the Word of God is to be taught. The word Χριστιανός is only used three times in Bible. We will examine all three instances here.

In Acts 16:31, Paul gives witness to a Roman jailer, telling him, "Believe in the Lord Jesus and you will be saved, you and your household." We see this confirmed in the tenth chapter of Romans (we discussed it in the last chapter, go back and read Romans 10:4-

10). The disciples giving their testimony of Jesus to the people around them becomes a key signature of the Christian. When he is before King Agrippa in the twenty-sixth chapter of Acts, Paul tells the king first about his actions before coming to know Christ (openly defying and attacking the disciples of Christ), then his deliverance in hearing from Jesus, seen in Acts 26:14-18 (BSB):

> We all fell to the ground, and I heard a voice say to me in Hebrew, 'Saul, Saul, why do you persecute Me? It is hard for you to kick against the goads.'
>
> 'Who are You, Lord?' I asked.
>
> 'I am Jesus, whom you are persecuting,' the Lord replied. 'But get up and stand on your feet. For I have appeared to you to appoint you as a servant and as a witness of what you have seen from Me and what I will show you. I will rescue you from your own people and from the Gentiles. I am sending you to them to open their eyes, so that they may turn from darkness to light and from the power of Satan to God, that they may receive forgiveness of sins and an inheritance among those sanctified by faith in Me.'

This in turn becomes the message Paul preached. Paul preaches this message to much of the known world before ending up in front of King Agrippa. We see the conversation between Paul and Agrippa reach a climax in verse 28 and 29 (BSB):

> Then Agrippa said to Paul, "Can you persuade me in such a short time to become a **Christian**?"
>
> "Short time or long," Paul replied, "I wish to God that not only you but all who hear me this day may become what I am, except for these chains."

The second mention of the word "Christian" here is not someone meekly talking about Jesus in the cover of darkness, but instead a person making a bold profession of faith in front of a non-believing ruler of the day. More than that, Paul says specifically he desires that, "all who hear me this day," would become a Christ follower. So more than someone who preaches and speaks the message of Christ, a Christian is to become like Paul is, boldly professing the truth of Christ in front of all.

Paul had a divine revelation of Jesus without personally knowing Jesus. Peter walked with Jesus before the resurrection. Both men, however, were brought to similar revelations, through the Holy Spirit, of what a Christ follower is to be. In 1 Peter 4:12-19 (BSB), Peter is giving the church a glimpse of what to expect:

> Beloved, do not be surprised at the fiery trial that has come upon you, as though something strange were happening to you. But rejoice that you share in the sufferings of Christ, so that you may be overjoyed at the revelation of His glory.
>
> If you are insulted for the name of Christ, you are blessed, because the Spirit of glory and of God rests on you. Indeed, none of you should suffer as a murderer or thief or wrongdoer, or even as a meddler. But if you suffer as a **Christian**, do not be ashamed, but glorify God that you bear that name. For it is time for judgment to begin with the family of God; and if it begins with us, what will the outcome be for those who disobey the gospel of God? And,
>
> "If it is hard for the righteous to be saved,
> what will become of the ungodly and the sinner?"
>
> So then, those who suffer according to God's will should entrust their souls to their faithful Creator and continue to do good.

In John 3:17-18 (BSB), we saw that the natural state of the world is condemnation and that, "God did not send His Son into the world to judge and condemn the world, but to be its Savior and rescue it!" This condemnation that is in the world does not come from God and so the followers of God will likely find themselves coming against it. Peter in the above verses tells us that we can pretty well assume that we will face challenges for being a Christ follower. Notice *how* we are to respond to these challenges, "But rejoice that you share in the sufferings of Christ, so that you may be overjoyed at the revelation of His glory." Rejoice that you may be overjoyed. How can someone rejoice in suffering? The last few verses tell us clearly that our joy is not looking to the present where there is suffering, but to the coming judgment. This response of rejoicing when faced with suffering can also be seen back in the first chapter (1 Peter 1:3-7, BSB):

> Blessed be the God and Father of our Lord Jesus Christ! By His great mercy He has given us new birth into a living hope through the resurrection of Jesus Christ from the dead, and into an inheritance that is imperishable, undefiled, and unfading, reserved in heaven for you, who through faith are shielded by God's power for the salvation that is ready to be revealed in the last time.
>
> In this you greatly rejoice, though now for a little while you may have had to suffer grief in various trials so that the proven character of your faith—more precious than gold, which perishes even though refined by fire—may result in praise, glory, and honor at the revelation of Jesus Christ.

The grief that the church suffered proved the character of their faith, resulting in praise, glory and honor to God. Notice the phrase, "at the revelation of Jesus Christ." These scattered people to whom Peter wrote this letter gained a deeper revelation of Jesus in their sufferings. Why would that be the case? Verse three points back to "His great mercy." The mercy or 'checed' of God allows us to gain a deeper revelation of who Christ is through suffering. Paul wrote similarly in Romans 5:3 which we investigated in the last chapter. In the Passion Translation (TPT), Romans 5:2-5 reads as:

> Our faith guarantees us permanent access into this marvelous kindness that has given us a perfect relationship with God. What incredible joy bursts forth within us as we keep on celebrating our hope of experiencing God's glory!

> But that's not all! Even in times of trouble we have a joyful confidence, knowing that our pressures will develop in us patient endurance. And patient endurance will refine our character, and proven character leads us back to hope. And hope is not a disappointing fantasy, because we can now experience the endless love of God cascading into our hearts through the Holy Spirit who lives in us!

In troubles, who do we turn to? If we are turning to God, relying upon Jesus, we have this "joyful confidence" welling up within us. Even in times of trouble we can "experience the endless love of God cascading into our hearts through the Holy Spirit." But where is this source of joy? The last sentence of verse two reveals to us, "what incredible joy bursts forth within us as we keep on celebrating our hope of experiencing God's glory." It is in the celebration of God and the hope of experiencing His glory. Notice that joy here is not attributed to the act of experiencing God's glory, but the hope of that experience. People often confuse "joy" for "happiness." This biblical joy is in "knowing that our pressures will develop in us patient endurance," it is a means of spiritual development.

Joy is often connected to praise. The Psalms in particular point to the interconnectedness of both joy and praise: Psalm 27:6 (KJV), "And now shall mine head be lifted up above mine enemies round about me: therefore will I offer in his tabernacle sacrifices of joy; I will sing, yea, I will sing praises unto the LORD." Psalm 33:1 (NLT), "Let the godly sing for joy to the LORD; it is fitting for the pure to praise him." Psalm 63:5 (BSB), "My soul is satisfied as with the richest of foods; with joyful lips my mouth will praise You." In each of these examples, there is a remembrance of how good the LORD is to His people. To be joyful is not to be happy, rather to be reflective and grateful for what the LORD has done, is doing, and will do in your life.

Jesus teaches His disciples about this joy in what is referred to as the "Last Supper," the covenant meal with His disciples prior to His crucifixion. John 16:23-24 (BSB) gives the following:

In that day you will no longer ask Me anything. Truly, truly, I tell you, whatever you ask the Father in My name, He will give you. Until now you have not asked for anything in My name. Ask and you will receive, so that your joy may be complete.

In these verses, Jesus teaches us two things: 1) how to pray and 2) why to pray. Jesus teaches us to pray *to* the Father *in* the Name of Jesus. This is often misconstrued with people praying *to* Jesus but that is not what He taught and it is not biblical. Why we would pray is clear: to receive. To be clear, there are many forms of prayer but if the prayer takes the form of asking, there is a guarantee of receiving. [Consider Matthew 7:7-8 (BSB), "Ask, and it will be given to you; seek, and you will find; knock, and the door will be opened to you. For everyone who asks receives; he who seeks finds; and to him who knocks, the door will be opened," also Luke 11:9-10 (BSB), "So I tell you: Ask, and it will be given to you; seek, and you will find; knock, and the door will be opened to you. For everyone who asks receives; he who seeks finds; and to him who knocks, the door will be opened," as well as Mark 11:24.] There are many conditions on prayer that we will discuss later in this chapter but Jesus points out that His disciples did not ask in His Name but if they were to henceforth, they would receive and the result therein would be that their joy would be complete. That joy, as we saw in Romans, comes in hope. Jesus tells His disciples why they should hope at the end of John 16, in the thirty-third verse (BSB), "I have told you these things so that in Me you may have peace. In the world you will have tribulation. But take courage; I have overcome the world!" Christ followers can have hope because Jesus has overcome the world!

Putting this together we see a Christian is a person who believes in their heart that Jesus was raised from the dead by God and then professes this belief to others. A Christian will face trials and tribulations because there is condemnation in this world but the Christian is not of this world. Christians are to grow in their relationship with the Father through persevering in hard times and setting a hopeful expectation for what is to come as God's glory. Growing in the hopeful expectation of God's glory is seen in purposeful practice of prayer.

Chapter 18 - Purposeful Practice of Prayer

There are literally hundreds of books on prayer, covering the types of prayer, the conditions for prayer, and "why prayer fails," an ever ominous title one can assume is meant to catch the eye of the concerned Christian. We will do a surface level study, an introduction. Should the LORD lead, another book will be written. For now, let us review what we have already discussed in the previous chapters in the following points:

1) **Prayer is important**: Jesus taught prayer and actively engaged in it Himself. If it is important for Him, it should be important for us.
2) **Prayer is to the Father**: John 16:23. We will investigate what is referred to as "The LORD's Prayer" later on.
3) **Prayer should be in the Name of Jesus**: We have read countless verses on the importance and power of the Name of Jesus and the miracles worked through that name. Notice that prior to the covenant meal, Jesus does not teach His disciples to pray in His name (John 16:23-24).
4) **Prayer requires believing**: Mark 11:23-24.
5) **Prayer must come from a place of forgiveness**: Mark 11:25 and "The LORD's Prayer," see also our in-depth study on forgiveness in chapter 3.

In starting this section on prayer, we will start with what the Master taught the disciples in Matthew 6 in what is referred to as the Sermon on the Mount (discussed in chapter 1). We will take up Matthew 6:5-15 in the New Living Translation (NLT) as our first piece of text to study in-depth from Scripture:

> "When you pray, don't be like the hypocrites who love to pray publicly on street corners and in the synagogues where everyone can see them. I tell you the truth, that is all the reward they will ever get. But when you pray, go away by yourself, shut the door behind you, and pray to your Father in private. Then your Father, who sees everything, will reward you.
>
> "When you pray, don't babble on and on as the Gentiles do. They think their prayers are answered merely by repeating their words again and again. Don't be like them, for your Father knows exactly what you need even before you ask him! Pray like this:
>
> Our Father in heaven,
> may your name be kept holy.
> May your Kingdom come soon.
> May your will be done on earth,

> as it is in heaven.
> Give us today the food we need,
> and forgive us our sins,
> as we have forgiven those who sin against us.
> And don't let us yield to temptation,
> but rescue us from the evil one.
>
> "If you forgive those who sin against you, your heavenly Father will forgive you. But if you refuse to forgive others, your Father will not forgive your sins."

Starting with the words, "Our Father," we have what is referred to as "The LORD's Prayer," a very well-known prayer used in various denominations of Christianity and clearly has biblical backing. We are to pray to the LORD as Father and exalt His Name at the start of the prayer. Jesus often spoke of the LORD as Father (as His first and to be accepted as ours as well). The Old Testament is thick with the importance of the Name of the LORD, like 1 Chronicles 22:7 when David is telling Solomon of his desire to build the first temple for God (BSB), "'My son,' said David to Solomon, "it was in my heart to build a house for the Name of the LORD my God…'" The prayer continues with the agreement with Jesus that the kingdom of God would come soon and praying that the Will of the LORD would be done now "on earth as it is in heaven." There is a spot for petition, "give us today the food we need," understanding that tomorrow is not guaranteed. The next section is very important and later in this book we will dig deeper into this presented concept: forgiveness. Next is the asking not to be led into temptation, just like in Jabez's prayer to the LORD in 1 Chronicles 4:10 (KJV), "And Jabez called on the God of Israel, saying, Oh that thou wouldest bless me indeed, and enlarge my coast, and that thine hand might be with me, and that thou wouldest keep *me* from evil, that it may not grieve me! And God granted him that which he requested." Just as the request of Jabez was granted, so too are we promised the granting of our promises when we pray in faith, in the Name of the LORD, and in a state of forgiveness.

Notice also that Jesus had not died so He had neither given wide use of His Name, nor the Holy Spirit to indwell the believer. We see that in His first teaching on prayer, Jesus speaks to the importance of forgiveness as we saw in Mark 11. Notice the first two paragraphs. Jesus tells us how to pray in contrast to what the Pharisees and religious leaders of the day were doing. Jesus says to pray in private and to pray to the point. Matthew 6:7 in the King James Version is given as, "But when ye pray, use not vain repetitions, as the heathen *do*: for they think that they shall be heard for their much speaking." Say what you need to say. Believe that as you pray, the LORD hears and will set to action according to your prayers not because of "much speaking" but because you pray in faith.

Similar to the verses given in Matthew 6, Luke 11:1-4 (BSB) includes an abbreviated version of this teaching to the disciples:

> One day in a place where Jesus had just finished praying, one of His disciples requested, "Lord, teach us to pray, just as John taught his disciples."
>
> So Jesus told them, "When you pray, say:
>
> 'Father, hallowed be Your name.
> Your kingdom come.
> Give us each day our daily bread.
> And forgive us our sins,
> for we also forgive everyone who sins against us.
> And lead us not into temptation.'"

The disciples had seen Jesus pray and wanted to know more about prayer themselves. What is of most interest in this account is not these verses but the parable Jesus uses afterwards in Luke 11:5-13 (BSB):

> Then Jesus said to them, "Suppose one of you goes to his friend at midnight and says, 'Friend, lend me three loaves of bread, because a friend of mine has come to me on a journey, and I have nothing to set before him.'
>
> And suppose the one inside answers, 'Do not bother me. My door is already shut, and my children and I are in bed. I cannot get up to give you anything.'
>
> I tell you, even though he will not get up to provide for him because of his friendship, yet because of the man's persistence, he will get up and give him as much as he needs.
>
> So I tell you: Ask, and it will be given to you; seek, and you will find; knock, and the door will be opened to you. For everyone who asks receives; he who seeks finds; and to him who knocks, the door will be opened.
>
> What father among you, if his son asks for a fish, will give him a snake instead? Or if he asks for an egg, will give him a scorpion? So if you who are evil know how to give good gifts to your children, how much more will your Father in heaven give the Holy Spirit to those who ask Him!"

In the last verse, Jesus connects the parable to asking the Father, much like the prayer He taught in verses two through four. Jesus attributes the man receiving "as much as he needs" not because of his friendship to his neighbor, but because of persistence.

Persistence carries with it the assumption of success. One who persistently knocks believes that the door will be opened if he knocks; one who persistently looks believes he will find what he seeks; one who persistently asks believes that the answer can and will be found. Jesus thereby teaches us that we have to be confident in our praying by being persistent.

Jesus teaches on persistence again in Luke 18:1-8 (BSB) through another parable:

> Then Jesus told them a parable about their need to pray at all times and not lose heart: "In a certain town there was a judge who neither feared God nor respected men. And there was a widow in that town who kept appealing to him, 'Give me justice against my adversary.'
>
> For a while he refused, but later he said to himself, 'Though I neither fear God nor respect men, yet because this widow keeps pestering me, I will give her justice. Then she will stop wearing me out with her perpetual requests.'"
>
> And the Lord said, "Listen to the words of the unjust judge. Will not God bring about justice for His elect who cry out to Him day and night? Will He continue to defer their help? I tell you, He will promptly carry out justice on their behalf. Nevertheless, when the Son of Man comes, will He find faith on earth?"

Jesus clearly teaches us through these parables that we are to pray continually. His last question in this verse should pique our interest: "Will He find faith on earth?" Jesus says that those who cry out to Him will have justice carried out for them but then asks about faith. Why?

We see that these three bits of Scripture (Matthew 6, Luke 11, and Luke 18) all have the commonality of persistence. Moreover, this is the persistence of someone who believes that something will be done about their situation. That is faith! Mark 11:22 again is "Have faith in God!" The Douay-Rheims Bible (DRB) has a more literal rendering of this verse as "Have the faith of God!" Mark 11:22-24 in the DRB then is given as, 'And Jesus answering, saith to them: "Have the **faith** of God. Amen I say to you, that whosoever shall say to this mountain, Be thou removed and be cast into the sea, and shall not stagger in his heart, but **believe**, that whatsoever he saith shall be done; it shall be done unto him. Therefore I say unto you, all things, whatsoever you ask when ye pray, **believe** that you shall receive; and they shall come unto you." ' Notice the contrast here between faith and believe: Have faith (a noun) and believe (a verb). Rather than build a case for either word, consider them as a "confident assurance," with faith in the noun form and believe in the verb form. Instead, look to another word that Jesus uses in this statement that is important for our study of prayer.

Looking at Mark 11:22-25 (DRB), a different word is bolded for emphasis to show the power of what you say, 'And Jesus answering, saith to them: "Have the faith of God. Amen I **say** to you, that whosoever shall **say** to this mountain, Be thou removed and be cast into the sea, and shall not stagger in his heart, but believe, that whatsoever he **saith** shall be done; it shall be done unto him. Therefore I **say** unto you, all things, whatsoever you **ask** when ye pray, believe that you shall receive; and they shall come unto you."' Notice that as opposed to the two times "believe" is used, Jesus uses words like "ask" and "say" five times! This should bring revelation to us that prayer is not quiet contemplation. Prayer is not done in thought only. To pray as Jesus taught, we must say! Notice earlier in this section Jesus speaks to praying behind closed doors (Matthew 6:5-6, BSB). Why would it matter where you pray if we did it silently every time? Or as Jesus states in Matthew 6:7, the answers of the pagans would not be "heard?" These each seem to indicate that our prayers are to be audible.

Chapter 19 - Why We Pray

There are many reasons to pray. One such reason we see in the previous section has to do with asking. We can ask of the Father in the Name of Jesus and we can expect to receive. It is important to identify that the verses above could be taken to speak about our praying for ourselves and praying for others. In this section, we will dig into the latter form of prayer, often referred to as intercessory prayer. An intercessor is someone who intervenes for someone else. Let us look at some biblical examples of intercession, starting with the last prayer Jesus prays at the covenant meal before His betrayal in the garden, specifically John 17:9-23 (BSB):

> I ask on their behalf. I do not ask on behalf of the world, but on behalf of those You have given Me; for they are Yours. All I have is Yours, and all You have is Mine; and in them I have been glorified. I will no longer be in the world, but they are in the world, and I am coming to You.
>
> Holy Father, protect them by Your name, the name You gave Me, so that they may be one as We are one. While I was with them, I protected and preserved them by Your name, the name You gave Me. Not one of them has been lost, except the son of destruction, so that the Scripture would be fulfilled.
>
> But now I am coming to You; and I am saying these things while I am in the world, so that they may have My joy fulfilled within them. I have given them Your word and the world has hated them; for they are not of the world, just as I am not of the world.
>
> I am not asking that You take them out of the world, but that You keep them from the evil one. They are not of the world, just as I am not of the world. Sanctify them by the truth; Your word is truth. As You sent Me into the world, I have also sent them into the world. For them I sanctify Myself, so that they too may be sanctified by the truth.
>
> I am not asking on behalf of them alone, but also on behalf of those who will believe in Me through their message, that all of them may be one, as You, Father, are in Me, and I am in You. May they also be in Us, so that the world may believe that You sent Me.
>
> I have given them the glory You gave Me, so that they may be one as We are one— I in them and You in Me—that they may be perfectly united, so that the world may know that You sent Me and have loved them just as You have loved Me.

In this portion of His prayer, Jesus states that He is asking on "their behalf," specifying His disciples. He adds that He is interceding not only for His disciples but on "behalf of those who **will** believe in Me through their message." So this type of prayer must specify the beneficiary of the prayer (including those who are affected by events that have not yet happened since the word "will" and not "have" was used).

This prayer makes two requests with justifications for those requests: 1) protection of the believer in the Name of the LORD and 2) sanctification from the evil one. Jesus uses the verse, "Holy Father, protect them by Your name, the name You gave Me, so that they may be one as We are one," to ensure our protection to produce unity. Jesus desires that we be one as He and the Father are one. Notice that this is to produce something in us, "I am saying these things while I am in the world, so that they may have My joy fulfilled within them." Our protection and our unity as one body of believers is to produce joy within us! We can see also that this unity among believers, in Jesus, in the Father, is to result in the world believing that the Father sent Jesus. Our unity is to have an impact in the lives of the people around us so they will see the working of the LORD in action in Jesus. The second request is given by these verses, "I am not asking that You take them out of the world, but that You keep them from the evil one. They are not of the world, just as I am not of the world. Sanctify them by the truth; Your word is truth. As You sent Me into the world, I have also sent them into the world. For them I sanctify Myself, so that they too may be sanctified by the truth." This shows us that the "keeping from the evil one" is done through sanctification by the truth. The word for sanctify is also translated as "make holy" or "set apart." You can see this in the use of the phrase "they are not of the world." We are to live in the world, but not of the world. Jesus sets a precedent right here in this intercessory prayer to call us to be set apart, much as we discussed in our first chapter.

It is important to distinguish what Jesus is praying for with what He states is already done. He does not ask the Father to give us His glory. Jesus specifies that He gave us His glory and in that glory, we have unity, we are in Jesus and Jesus is in the Father. The glory of Jesus, as can be seen by His grace, is ours. Pray for protection, pray for a setting aside, but we have the miracle working power of God, His glory, already given to us by the Father through Jesus.

Paul in His epistles gives us a demonstration of the kind of prayer life we are to live by constantly citing his prayer for the churches and the believers in them. Consider 1 Thessalonians 1:2-3 (BSB), "We always thank God for all of you, remembering you in our prayers and continually recalling before our God and Father your work of faith, your labor of love, and your enduring hope in our Lord Jesus Christ." Paul thanks God for each of the believers, remembering them in his prayers. Paul also calls on the works of faith, hope and love done in Jesus to the Father. How important it is that we too should thank God and remember others in our prayers for their actions that demonstrate faith, hope and love. In 1 Thessalonians 5:16-25 (NLT), Paul give the following direction to the church:

> Always be joyful. Never stop praying. Be thankful in all circumstances, for this is God's will for you who belong to Christ Jesus.
>
> Do not stifle the Holy Spirit. Do not scoff at prophecies, but test everything that is said. Hold on to what is good. Stay away from every kind of evil.
>
> Now may the God of peace make you holy in every way, and may your whole spirit and soul and body be kept blameless until our Lord Jesus Christ comes again. God will make this happen, for he who calls you is faithful.
>
> Dear brothers and sisters, pray for us.

Notice how each of these sections are grouped: 1) be ever joyful through continually praying and thankfulness in all things, 2) work with the Holy Spirit, not against Him, 3) God will help you in being holy through His peace, and 4) pray for others, including those who pray for you. Praying is to be a reciprocal relationship. God has not called us to be those who only receive prayer, but also those who partake in prayer for the support of our fellow believer.

We see this also in Paul's letter to the church in Colossae, a church Paul had not even visited! Colossians 1:3-14 (BSB) gives us the following:

> We always thank God, the Father of our Lord Jesus Christ, when we pray for you, because we have heard about your faith in Christ Jesus and your love for all the saints— the faith and love proceeding from the hope stored up for you in heaven, of which you have already heard in the word of truth, the gospel that has come to you.
>
> All over the world this gospel is bearing fruit and growing, just as it has been doing among you since the day you heard it and truly understood the grace of God. You learned it from Epaphras, our beloved fellow servant, who is a faithful minister of Christ on our behalf, and who also informed us of your love in the Spirit.

[Notice these first two sections identify that Paul had not personally preached to them.]

> For this reason, since the day we heard about you, we have not stopped praying for you and asking God to fill you with the knowledge of His will in all spiritual wisdom and understanding, so that you may walk in a manner worthy of the Lord and may please Him in every way: bearing fruit in every good work, growing in the

> knowledge of God, being strengthened with all power according to His glorious might so that you may have full endurance and patience, and joyfully giving thanks to the Father, who has qualified you to share in the inheritance of the saints in the light.
>
> He has rescued us from the dominion of darkness and brought us into the kingdom of His beloved Son, in whom we have redemption, the forgiveness of sins.

Paul mentions four key things in this prayer: 1) Paul is praying continually, 2) Paul asks that God fill these believers with the knowledge of His will, 3) Paul prays that the believers would walk in a manner worthy of the LORD, and that 4) the believers would please the LORD in every way. For our benefit, Paul gives some key metrics for a person who is growing in the knowledge of the will of God, walking in a manner worthy of and pleasing to God. These include bearing fruit in every good work (fruit is evidence of growth), growing in the knowledge of God (never being content with what you already know about Him), strengthened by His might to have endurance and patience (His strength produces in us the ability to power through tough situations), and joyful giving (not just joy, not just giving). At the end of his letter to Colossae, Paul again talks about prayer, though this time it is directions for prayer. Colossians 4:2-4 (BSB):

> Devote yourselves to prayer, being watchful and thankful, as you pray also for us, that God may open to us a door for the word, so that we may proclaim the mystery of Christ, for which I am in chains. Pray that I may declare it clearly, as I should.

We are to devote ourselves to prayer, praying that the Word of God would be revealed to those who do not yet know it and that it would find its way through when it is being blocked. Our adversary, the devil, does not want the Word of God revealed to the world so he endeavors to hinder it anyway he can. The devil also desires that we would not pray. We see that in these various verses, we are encouraged to pray continually or without ceasing. This is because the manifestation of a prayer brings forth joy and faith. If we become weak in either of these areas, the devil can take the Word from us, leaving us exposed and susceptible to harm.

We see that there are many things to pray for that produce growth in us as believers. It is also biblical for us to pray to remove illness from a fellow believer. Consider James' direction given in James 5:13-18 (BSB):

> Is any one of you suffering? He should pray. Is anyone cheerful? He should sing praises. Is any one of you sick? He should call the elders of the church to pray over him and anoint him with oil in the name of the Lord. And the prayer offered in faith

will restore the one who is sick. The Lord will raise him up. If he has sinned, he will be forgiven.

Therefore confess your sins to each other and pray for each other so that you may be healed. The prayer of a righteous man has great power to prevail. Elijah was a man just like us. He prayed earnestly that it would not rain, and it did not rain on the land for three and a half years. Again he prayed, and the heavens gave rain, and the earth yielded its crops.

Notice three questions with three answers, all requiring an action of the believer and delivering something to God in the form of prayer or praise. This response of God hearing the prayer of the righteous or hearing the praise of His people and responding is found throughout the Bible. Consider Job. The story of Job is well known and often celebrated for the wrong reasons; people often quote what Job or his friends say throughout the story and use it as "sage wisdom." At the end of the book of Job, Job hears from God, understands his fault, and says (Job 42:6, BSB), "Therefore I retract my words, and I repent in dust and ashes." Job repents. His friends, however, must do a bit more to satisfy the LORD. Job 42:7-12 (BSB) gives us the following:

After the LORD had spoken these words to Job, He said to Eliphaz the Temanite, "My wrath is kindled against you and your two friends. For you have not spoken about Me accurately, as My servant Job has. So now, take seven bulls and seven rams, go to My servant Job, and sacrifice a burnt offering for yourselves. Then My servant Job will **pray** for you, for I will accept his **prayer** and not deal with you according to your folly. For you have not spoken accurately about Me, as My servant Job has."

So Eliphaz the Temanite, Bildad the Shuhite, and Zophar the Naamathite went and did as the LORD had told them; and the LORD accepted Job's request.

After Job had **prayed** for his friends, the LORD restored his prosperity and doubled his former possessions. All his brothers and sisters and prior acquaintances came and dined with him in his house. They consoled him and comforted him over all the adversity that the LORD had brought upon him. And each one gave him a piece of silver and a gold ring.

So the LORD blessed Job's latter days more than his first…

Job prayed for his friends. It is after these words that the blessings of God come back onto Job. Job had already repented but in his praying for his friends, giving this sacrifice to the LORD, Job is putting himself in a place to receive from God. Everything was taken from Job throughout the book, but in the end, "the LORD blessed Job's latter days more than his first." What does this have to do with us as believers in Christ? In Hebrews 13:15-16 (BSB), we see that we are to offer a different sacrifice to God:

> Through Jesus, therefore, let us continually offer to God a sacrifice of praise, the fruit of lips that confess His name. And do not neglect to do good and to share with others, for with such sacrifices God is pleased.

So we see that we are to pray continually as well as continually offer to God our "sacrifice of praise." It is our duty to pray to God, both for ourselves and for those around us, both believer and unbeliever. We will end this section by looking at Paul's first letter to Timothy and the church he leads at Ephesus. In 1 Timothy 2:1-8 in the Contemporary English Version (CEV), we read:

> First of all, I ask you to pray for everyone. Ask God to help and bless them all, and tell God how thankful you are for each of them. Pray for kings and others in power, so we may live quiet and peaceful lives as we worship and honor God. This kind of prayer is good, and it pleases God our Savior. God wants everyone to be saved and to know the whole truth, which is,

> There is only one God,
> and Christ Jesus
> is the only one
> who can bring us
> to God.
> Jesus was truly human,
> and he gave himself
> to rescue all of us.
> God showed us this
> at the right time.

> This is why God chose me to be a preacher and an apostle of the good news. I am telling the truth. I am not lying. God sent me to teach the Gentiles about faith and truth.

> I want everyone everywhere to lift innocent hands toward heaven and pray, without being angry or arguing with each other.

We are to pray for our leaders, regardless of their political affiliation or their beliefs. We have seen guidance on who to pray for and how to pray as well as some reasons to pray. Sometimes, though, we find ourselves in a position where we do not know what to say in our prayers. What we must investigate is a phrase spoken many times by Paul, "praying in the Spirit."

Chapter 20 - Praying in the Holy Spirit

A highly contested aspect of the New Testament is the role the Holy Spirit plays in prayer. It is shown to us in Acts 2:1-4 (BSB) an example of the power the Holy Spirit brings in granting the ability to speak in other tongues to the disciples after the resurrection of Jesus:

> When the day of Pentecost came, they were all together in one place. Suddenly a sound like a mighty rushing wind came from heaven and filled the whole house where they were sitting. They saw tongues like flames of fire that separated and came to rest on each of them. And they were all filled with the Holy Spirit and began to speak in other tongues as the Spirit enabled them.
>
> Now there were dwelling in Jerusalem God-fearing Jews from every nation under heaven. And when this sound rang out, a crowd came together in bewilderment, because each one heard them speaking his own language.
>
> Astounded and amazed, they asked, "Are not all these men who are speaking Galileans? How is it then that each of us hears them in his own native language? Parthians, Medes, and Elamites; residents of Mesopotamia, Judea and Cappadocia, Pontus and Asia, Phrygia and Pamphylia, Egypt and the parts of Libya near Cyrene; visitors from Rome, both Jews and converts to Judaism; Cretans and Arabs—we hear them declaring the wonders of God in our own tongues!"

Notice that when filled with the Holy Spirit, each of these disciples were able to "speak in other tongues as the Spirit enabled them." In this case, each of the Jews present heard the speaking in their own language. Without knowing in their mind, these disciples were given the ability through their spirit by God's spirit to preach the gospel to the people around them. Peter confirms that this is not an accident but was foretold by the prophet Joel in Acts 2:14-21 (BSB):

> Then Peter stood up with the Eleven, lifted up his voice, and addressed the crowd: "Men of Judea and all who dwell in Jerusalem, let this be known to you, and listen carefully to my words. These men are not drunk, as you suppose. It is only the third hour of the day! No, this is what was spoken by the prophet Joel:
>
> 'In the last days, God says, I will pour out My Spirit on all people. Your sons and daughters will prophesy, your young men will see visions, your old men will dream dreams. Even on My menservants and maidservants I will pour out My Spirit in those days, and they will prophesy. I will show wonders in the heavens above and signs on the earth below, blood and fire and billows of smoke. The sun will be

turned to darkness, and the moon to blood, before the coming of the great and glorious Day of the Lord. And everyone who calls on the name of the Lord will be saved.'

God, through Joel, revealed that a time would come that the Spirit of God would be poured out for all people. Jesus tells His disciples, in fact, that the reason they were waiting here at this place was to receive the Holy Spirit. Not that they could not receive the Holy Spirit elsewhere, but that the Jews from other provinces would testify to the miracle of speaking in other tongues. In Acts 1:4-5 (BSB), we read:

> And while they were gathered together, He commanded them: "Do not leave Jerusalem, but wait for the gift the Father promised, which you have heard Me discuss. For John baptized with water, but in a few days you will be baptized with the Holy Spirit."

The disciples, therefore, received the Holy Spirit through a baptism. This baptism differs from the baptism of water. In Acts 8:14-18 (BSB), we see another contrast between these two baptisms:

> When the apostles in Jerusalem heard that Samaria had received the word of God, they sent Peter and John to them. On their arrival, they prayed for them to receive the Holy Spirit. For the Holy Spirit had not yet fallen upon any of them; they had simply been baptized into the name of the Lord Jesus. Then Peter and John laid their hands on them, and they received the Holy Spirit.
>
> When Simon saw that the Spirit was given through the laying on of the apostles' hands, he offered them money.

In the case of these Samarian disciples, they received the Holy Spirit through a laying on of hands. Contrast that with how the 120 received the Holy Spirit in the upper room. This tells us that the baptism of the Holy Spirit can be received by a few methods. Another example is the message preached by Peter after he meets Paul and has a revelation that the message they are to preach is not to Jews alone but to everyone. Acts 10:34-48 (BSB) gives the following account:

> Then Peter began to speak: "I now truly understand that God does not show favoritism, but welcomes those from every nation who fear Him and do what is right. He has sent this message to the people of Israel, proclaiming the gospel of peace through Jesus Christ, who is Lord of all.

You yourselves know what has happened throughout Judea, beginning in Galilee with the baptism that John proclaimed: how God anointed Jesus of Nazareth with the Holy Spirit and with power, and how Jesus went around doing good and healing all who were oppressed by the devil, because God was with Him.

We are witnesses of all that He did, both in the land of the Jews and in Jerusalem. And although they put Him to death by hanging Him on a tree, God raised Him up on the third day and caused Him to be seen— not by all the people, but by the witnesses God had chosen beforehand, by us who ate and drank with Him after He rose from the dead. And He commanded us to preach to the people and to testify that He is the One appointed by God to judge the living and the dead. All the prophets testify about Him that everyone who believes in Him receives forgiveness of sins through His name."

While Peter was still speaking these words, the Holy Spirit fell upon all who heard his message. All the circumcised believers who had accompanied Peter were astounded that the gift of the Holy Spirit had been poured out even on the Gentiles. For they heard them speaking in tongues and exalting God.

Then Peter said, "Can anyone withhold the water to baptize these people? They have received the Holy Spirit just as we have!" So he ordered that they be baptized in the name of Jesus Christ. Then they asked him to stay for a few days.

Look at Peter's statement towards the end, "Can anyone withhold the water to baptize these people?" This means that the people to whom Peter was teaching and preaching were not yet baptized by water. Furthermore, the section above the last one makes it clear that these people were uncircumcised as the disciples were, "astounded that the gift of the Holy Spirit had been poured out even on the Gentiles." How did these people receive the Holy Spirit? We read clearly that what happened was, "while Peter was still speaking these words, the Holy Spirit fell upon all who heard his message." Peter, preaching the Good News of salvation through Christ Jesus enabled the people to receive the Holy Spirit. We see, therefore, that in accepting Jesus Christ as your LORD and hearing the word preached can result in the receiving of the Holy Spirit.

In the eleventh chapter of Acts, Peter is confronted with a group of believers who challenge Peter's communing with the uncircumcised, a chiding not unlike what Jesus had received in His day. Peter recounts the story we read above and the prophecy Jesus reveals that they too would receive the Spirit of God (Acts 11:15-18, BSB):

> As I began to speak, the Holy Spirit fell upon them, just as He had fallen upon us at the beginning. Then I remembered the word of the Lord, as He used to say, 'John baptized with water, but you will be baptized with the Holy Spirit.' So if God gave them the same gift He gave us who believed in the Lord Jesus Christ, who was I to hinder the work of God?"
>
> When they heard this, their objections were put to rest, and they glorified God, saying, "So then, God has granted even the Gentiles repentance unto life."

This put to rest any contention among the believers. Yet how much contention do we see in our churches today? How many churches ignore the workings of the Spirit and denounce praying in tongues or prophecy? Paul would end his letter to the Ephesian church asking for prayer, specifically in the Spirit (Ephesians 6:18-20, NLT):

> Pray in the Spirit at all times and on every occasion. Stay alert and be persistent in your prayers for all believers everywhere.
>
> And pray for me, too. Ask God to give me the right words so I can boldly explain God's mysterious plan that the Good News is for Jews and Gentiles alike. I am in chains now, still preaching this message as God's ambassador. So pray that I will keep on speaking boldly for him, as I should.

Paul would urge us to pray in the Spirit, "at all times and on every occasion." If it was good for the early church, then it must be good for us. The Bible, written by man through the guidance of the Holy Spirit, is a message that stands outside of time. It speaks of matters for a people regardless of "when" they are. The New Testament speaks to those who believe in Jesus Christ as LORD, whether that be the first century believer or the twenty-first century believer. Paul's message is as pertinent then as it is now. Notice he even shows us that we can pray for others to have the right words and to speak boldly.

Chapter fourteen in the first letter to the Corinthians is a chapter regarding the proper usage of tongues and prophecy in a church service. Read the chapter and meditate on it, identifying what agrees with what we have discussed even if it challenges dogma commonly taught. Remember that when considering how to go about our lives as Christians: compare choices and teachings to the Word of God, choosing it over religious doctrine.

Before moving on to discuss the body of the church more in-depth, let us examine 1 Corinthians 14:34-35 (TPT) which are verses that have been abused by congregations in the past or by people to refute the value of the epistles:

The women[e] should be respectfully silent *during the evaluation of prophecy in the meetings.*[f] They are not allowed to interrupt,[g] but are to be in a support role, as in fact the law teaches.[h] If they want to inquire about something, let them ask their husbands when they get home, for a woman embarrasses herself when she constantly interrupts the church meeting.[i]

Footnotes:

e 14:34 Or "wives."

f 14:34 Implied in the greater context. The theme Paul is addressing is unity and mutual edification, not simply the role of women. Women are permitted to speak in church, to prophesy, and to minister the gospel. See 1 Cor. 11:2-16; 14:31. Paul is apparently prohibiting interrupting the leaders as they evaluate prophetic utterances. It is likely that Paul was addressing a specific issue taking place in the church fellowship of Corinth with women interrupting the meetings with their opinions and questions about the prophetic words just spoken, possibly even words spoken by their husbands.

g 14:34 Or "speak." Interrupting the meeting is implied when compared with 1 Cor. 11:2-16; 14:31; Acts 2:16-21; 21:9.

h 14:34 See Gen. 2:18-24; 3:16

i 14:35 One interpretation of this passage is that Paul is quoting from a letter written by the Corinthians to him. They were the ones saying a woman should remain silent and Paul is responding to their questions. In other words, they were imposing a rule in the church that Paul refers to in v. 36. Some manuscripts move vv. 34-35 to after v. 40, which causes a few scholars to consider this as evidence of an early introduction into the text by Jewish scribes. The only two places in the New Testament where Paul writes about women being quiet or not teaching in the church are in his letters to the church of Ephesus (1 Timothy) and Corinth. Both cities were centers of worship to the goddess Artemis (Diana), where women had the leading roles of teaching and temple prostitution was commonplace. To the Galatians Paul writes that there is no distinction between believing men and women (Gal. 3:28).

Whether these verses are a response to a letter from Corinth, a response to immoral acts of women of the region, or added at a later point by Jewish scribes, we can see that by examining context that they are not the focus of this part of Paul's letter, nor are they an assessment of how Paul views women. Considering that this first letter covers in-depth the sexual misconduct of one of the members of the church in Corinth as well as the indifference that the rest of the church seemed to show, it seems likely that Paul is addressing the misconceptions of the people, especially considering 1 Corinthians 14:36-40 (TPT):

> Do you actually think that you were the starting point for the Word of God going forth? Were you the only ones it was sent to? *I don't think so!* If anyone considers themselves to be a prophet or a spiritual person, let them discern that what I'm writing to you carries the Lord's authority. And if anyone continues not to recognize this, they should not be recognized!

> So, beloved friends, with all this in mind, be passionate to prophesy and don't forbid anyone from speaking in tongues, doing all things in a beautiful and orderly way.

Context is imperative in reading and interpreting the Scriptures. This is a large reason why we spent so much time discussing the covenant because each covenant has its own stipulations and relying on the wrong rules and regulations to govern your life can lead to issues for you and for others. As a reminder, the Old Covenant tenets around living in the Will of God pertain to your righteousness, your actions and how they impact your standing with God. New Covenant tenets for living in the Will of God pertain to Jesus' righteousness and how we are made righteous in our belief in Him. This belief in Jesus opens us up to the Holy Spirit so that the Spirit can work in and through us. The letter of Jude warns of those who will try and cause strife among believers, those who would bend the Word to fit their agenda. This little book located just before Revelation contains only one chapter, yet finds it of importance to mention, "praying in the Spirit." Jude 17-23 (TPT):

> But you, *my* delightfully loved friends, remember the prophecies of the apostles of our Lord Jesus, the Anointed One. They taught you, "In the last days[a] there will always be mockers, motivated by their own ungodly desires."[b] These people cause divisions and are followers of their own natural instincts, devoid of *the life of* the Spirit.

> But you, *my* delightfully loved friends, constantly and progressively build yourselves up on the foundation of your most holy faith[c] by praying every moment in the Spirit.[d] Fasten your hearts to the love of God and receive the mercy of our Lord Jesus Christ, who gives us eternal life.[e]

> Keep being compassionate to those who still have doubts,[f] and snatch others out of the fire to save them. Be merciful over and over to them, but always couple your

mercy with the fear of God. Be extremely careful to keep yourselves free from the pollutants of the flesh.g

Footnotes:

a 18 The last days began at Pentecost and have continued for more than two thousand years. We have been living in the last days since the Holy Spirit was poured out. See Acts 2:17; Heb. 1:2.

b 18 See Acts 20:29; 1 Tim. 4:1; 2 Tim. 3:1-5; 2 Peter 3:2-3; 2 John 7.

c 20 Or "faithfulness."

d 20 Paul uses the phrase "praying ... in the Spirit" to refer to praying in tongues. See Rom. 8:26; 1 Cor. 14:15; Eph. 6:18. It can also mean "pray as led in the Spirit's realm," or "pray by means of/power of the Spirit."

e 21 Or "By constantly and progressively building each other up on the foundation of your most holy faith, and by praying every moment in the Spirit's power, you will keep yourselves in the love of God, awaiting the mercy of our Lord Jesus, who gives eternal life."

f 22 Or "Show mercy to those who are still undecided."

g 23 Or "hating even the garment ['snake skin' or 'coating'] of the pollution of the flesh [the natural realm]." In other words, we do all we can to bring others to Christ, but not at the expense of becoming like them in ignoring sin. Jude, in closing, gives us seven commands: (1) Keep building up your inner life on the foundation of faith. (2) Pray in the Holy Spirit. (3) Fasten your life to the love of God. (4) Receive more mercy from our Lord Jesus Christ. (5) Have compassion on the wavering. (6) Share the gospel with those who are lost. (7) Hate any compromise that will stain our lives.

Here we see yet another disciple of Christ point to praying in the Spirit as a responsibility of the believer today. Note that this form of praying could be in other tongues as Paul described it or in other translations. We could understand what is written here to pray as the Spirit leads, in a tongue we understand but in a way guided by the witness God gives to our spirit. There are many ways to pray but we must see here that our duty as Christians is to take on the task of praying, both in other tongues and a language we know. For further discussion on "tongues," see Appendix - Tongues, Travailing, and Psalms.

Chapter 21 - The Church

We have seen that as a body of believers, it is imperative that we actively participate in prayer on a regular basis. So if prayer is to be done in the back room, out of the public eye, why is there such an importance around "going to church?" As we will investigate, the gathering together of believers is biblical. Furthermore, each believer is called to a specific role by being a part of "the church."

The word translated "church" is first seen in Matthew 16. Jesus is talking with His disciples about who the people of the region believe Him to be (Matthew 16:13-19, BSB):

> When Jesus came to the region of Caesarea Philippi, He questioned His disciples: "Who do people say the Son of Man is?"
>
> They replied, "Some say John the Baptist; others say Elijah; and still others, Jeremiah or one of the prophets."
>
> "But what about you?" Jesus asked. "Who do you say I am?"
>
> Simon Peter answered, "You are the Christ, the Son of the living God."
>
> Jesus replied, "Blessed are you, Simon son of Jonah! For this was not revealed to you by flesh and blood, but by My Father in heaven. And I tell you that you are Peter, and on this rock I will build My **church**, and the gates of Hades will not prevail against it. I will give you the keys of the kingdom of heaven. Whatever you bind on earth will be bound in heaven, and whatever you loose on earth will be loosed in heaven."

The word "church" is the Greek word '*ekklesia*' or ἐκκλησία which in both secular and biblical Greek texts refers to an "assembling together" (see Herodotus 3, 142 for a non-biblical usage). Note in particular that this "assembling together" will be built on a rock. Some theologians see this in the more literal sense that Peter is that rock (Peter coming from '*Petras*,' literally "rock") but context tells us that it is the revelation that Peter had, not Peter himself. Peter's revelation, from the Father, that Jesus is the Christ, the Son of the living God is the reason to gather. Furthermore, this assembly has a specific order to attack and be on the offensive as is seen by the phrase "the gates of Hades will not prevail against it." Think about that for a moment: there are gates to the place of the dead, Hades, but those gates will not prevail against the church. Gates are not an offensive force. Gates are purely defensive. The church has authority and power to come against the forces of the dead and be successful! The evidence that our warfare is spiritual but impacting the world, becomes more clear in the next sentence, "whatever you bind on earth will be bound in heaven, whatever you loose on earth will be loosed in heaven." Jesus explicitly connects the actions we do here on earth with a divine consequence. There still stands the question of *how* we are to "loose" or "bind."

We see the same words appear two chapters later in a section of Matthew 18 where Jesus is talking to His disciples about how they are to interact with each other. Matthew 18:15-20 (BSB) reads as:

> "If your brother sins against you, go and confront him privately. If he listens to you, you have won your brother over. But if he will not listen, take one or two others along, so that 'every matter may be established by the testimony of two or three witnesses.' If he refuses to listen to them, tell it to the church. And if he refuses to listen even to the church, regard him as you would a pagan or a tax collector. Truly I tell you, **whatever you bind on earth will be bound in heaven, and whatever you loose on earth will be loosed in heaven.** Again, I tell you truly that if two of you on the earth agree about anything you ask for, it will be done for you by My Father in heaven. For where two or three gather together in My name, there am I with them."

Bolded for emphasis are those same words from Matthew 16. What is interesting is the context in which Jesus states this phrase: first discussing how to handle a dispute and then asking in agreement. It is evident that Jesus desires that we live peaceably among other believers. However, we should note that if Jesus is going to outline a series of interventions in a dispute, it must be serious. If a brother or sister in the faith is refusing to repent of a wrong and correct their action against a fellow member of the same faith, they are to be regarded with contempt, "as you [a Jew] would regard a pagan or tax collector." Then after talking about loosing and binding, Jesus states "if two of you on the earth agree about anything you ask for…" Jesus reveals for us some important features of His Church, we are to forgive but strife and disagreement cannot reside within the Church. If these conditions are met, as believers pray, "it will be done for you by My Father in heaven." Furthermore, we have the 20th verse, "for where two or three gather together in My name, there am I with them." The assumption there would be that those believers are operating in forgiveness and in agreement.

The church is not a building, it is the body of believers. Moreover, this body of believers has a job to do, a war to fight. Victory is guaranteed, but the fight must still happen. This spiritual warfare, however, is not done only in isolation.

We are reminded in Hebrews 10:25 (BSB) to "not neglect meeting together, as some have made a habit, but let us encourage one another, and all the more as you see the Day approaching." We see that in us gathering together, we encourage one another. Even at the time this was written, people had fallen away from the practice of gathering together to worship Christ. Paul, in his letter to the Romans, talks of us as members of one body. Romans 12:3-8 (TPT) says the following:

> God has given me grace to speak a warning about pride. I would ask each of you to be emptied of self-promotion and not create a false image of your importance. Instead, honestly assess your worth by using your God-given faith as the standard of measurement, and then you will see your true value with an appropriate self-esteem.
>
> In the human body there are many parts and organs, each with a unique function. And so it is in the body of Christ. For though we are many, we've all been mingled into one body in Christ. This means that we are all vitally joined to one another, with each contributing to the others.
>
> God's marvelous grace imparts to each one of us varying gifts and ministries that are uniquely ours. So if God has given you the grace-gift of prophecy, you must activate your gift by using the proportion of faith you have to prophecy. If your grace-gift is serving, then thrive in serving others well. If you have the grace-gift of teaching, then be actively teaching and training others. If you have the grace-gift of encouragement, then use it often to encourage others. If you have the grace-gift of giving to meet the needs of others, then may you prosper in your generosity without any fanfare. If you have the gift of leadership, be passionate about your leadership. And if you have the gift of showing compassion, then flourish in your cheerful display of compassion.

We all have roles and duties to perform. In this section, Paul is not talking about the actual service of the church and positions of leadership within the church (see 1 Timothy 3). Instead, Paul is referring to each of us as "parts and organs." There is no part of the body that is non-essential to the appropriate and successful function of the body. Yet there is only one heart and only one brain in the human body. We each have duties to fulfill in the body of Christ, though that does not make us all leadership in the church. This is important to distinguish between roles and duties because we are called to have our own grace-gifts as Paul discusses in the last paragraph, grace-gifts that are "uniquely ours." Our discussion here is not to delve into each of these gifts but to identify that these are for members of the church, not simply pastors or deacons. The LORD imparts to each of us different gifts in different seasons of our lives. There may be times when we are to operate in a specific ministry gift (prophet, apostle, preacher, teacher, and evangelist, see Ephesians 4:11-13) and the anointing will flow as we operate in that gift within the Church, affecting the day-to-day operation of the Church. There may be times when we are to operate in what are referred to as "service gifts," prophecy, service, teaching, encouraging, giving, leading, and mercy (see Romans 12:3-8) which may affect the Church but are not for the explicit functioning of the Church. We are to be led by the Spirit of God as we move through these different gifts. It is our duty to operate in those giftings and not to give an excuse or explanation.

Our ministry is the means by which the LORD operates through us. One does not need to be the lead pastor or priest to have a ministry. Jesus called each and everyone of us to have a ministry when He gave His parting words before ascending into heaven, Matthew 28:19-20 (BSB), "Therefore go and make disciples of all nations, baptizing them in the name of the Father, and of the Son, and of the Holy Spirit, and teaching them to obey all that I have commanded you. And surely I am with you always, even to the end of the age." We each have been called to share the light of Christ with the world in our own way. In the same way that He sent the 12 and then the 70 to go forth and spread the Good News of deliverance, this final order sets us with the authority to do the same. There are people only you can reach through your unique giftings. There are some people who may never hear this message of grace if you do not bring it to them. There are some people who will hear this message countless times but the anointing of God will be on your lips as you deliver it again, the anointing that melts hearts of stone and brings revelation of who Jesus is. For too long, we as a body of believers have attributed evangelizing for someone else to do. The LORD does not call all of us to stand in front of crowds but His does call us to boldly proclaim the Truth to both believer and non-believer. For too long, we as a body of believers have "played church," put on fancy clothes, sang hymns, listened to a preacher or pastor, and then went back to our day unaffected. Our witnessing and sharing of the Gospel should have an effect! Jesus states in Mark 16:17-18 (BSB), "And these signs **will accompany those who believe**: In My name they will drive out demons; they will speak in new tongues; they will pick up snakes with their hands, and if they drink any deadly poison, it will not harm them; they will lay their hands on the sick, and they will be made well." Not "these signs will accompany those who went to seminary," not "these signs will accompany or preach on damnation," not "these signs will accompany those who passively listen to a sermon." The life of Christian boils down to belief. We must believe that we are new creatures in Christ, that we have a job to do by bringing wholeness to this broken world, and that we have the authority through Jesus to perform this job.

This is where we must reflect: am I living in and acting out the will of God for my life? As you ask yourself this question, consider your unique gifts: the ability to make someone smile, the ability to pick out just the right gift, the ability to say just the right words to give confident assurance to someone at work, the ability to bring peace to people in the midst of an argument. These are each gifts that people operate in outside of the church. Why not use them for the express purpose of sharing the light of Christ? Why not thank God for these gifts each and every moment, continually praising the glory and grace of God?

You may have a gift that will support you in leading a church. You may have a gift that will help you write a children's book. You may have a gift that allows you to have just the right faith-filled words in a secular place of work. Whatever special gifts we have been given by God, we are to use them and by using them, bring glory to God.

Regardless of our gifts, we Christians are all called to pray and to praise. In giving God our praise and lifting prayers up to Him, we lift up ourselves and those around us. If we lack anything, even clarity around our gifts, we are to ask the LORD and He will give us clarity when we ask in the Name of Jesus. There is still much to do for us as Christians in the world today. We must not belittle the roles we each must play to help spread the gospel to the people around us. We are to grow in our fellowship with God and with fellow believers. Let us not take for granted a person's salvation. There are many who attend a church or have heard the message of Jesus but have not made Him LORD. We are to pray for those around us, but we also must have honest conversations, not in the spirit of condemnation but genuine care for the world. Meditating on our discussion of who the Christian is and their responsibility in these the last days, let us pray for guidance:

> Father God in heaven, Your mercy endures forever! We pray that our joy and the joy of our fellow believers would be full, as it is our strength. We pray that those in authority, elected, appointed, or promoted would hear and heed the Word of God for it brings light and revelation. We pray that Your Hand be upon them, guiding and directing their decisions. Father, we welcome You into our hearts to stir a deeper revelation for what gifts You have given us. We ask that Your Holy Spirit which indwells us brings forth words to say as we pray and intercede for this hurting world around us. Open our eyes to the role You have for us in this world so that we may live and operate more fully in Your Will. All praise and glory are Yours, Almighty Father. It is in the blessed Name of Jesus we pray. Amen.

When a person is born again by making Jesus Christ the LORD of their life, Jesus sends His Spirit to reside on the inside of you. All born-again believers have the Holy Spirit already so there is no need to pray for Him. If you have not received the baptism of the Holy Spirit as evidenced by speaking in other tongues, pray this prayer and commit yourself to allowing the Spirit of God to speak through you:

> Father God, I believe with all of my heart that Jesus is the one way to You. I make Him the LORD of every aspect of my life and submit fully to Him. I receive now, through Your rich grace, the baptism of the Holy Spirit. I release Him to speak through my mouth and my vocal chords, speaking in languages known and unknown. I will not question or challenge the Holy Spirit but will confirm the words and works spoken by the Word of God. I thank You LORD that through Jesus Christ,

You count me worthy. I say now lips be loosed in the Name of Jesus. I speak now with my spirit and not with my mind. I glorify the Father for the gift of the Holy Spirit. I glorify God for His infinite grace. Thank you LORD. In Jesus Name I pray. Amen

The spirit of a man can be found in his belly. You may find a warm sensation in the region above your belly button. You may find a rising sensation that you cannot explain. People experience speaking in other tongues differently. The biggest obstacle to overcome is your own mind. People will often find themselves opening their mouth and not allowing the first sound to escape because they are trying to imagine what it should sound like. Receiving the baptism of the Holy Spirit is the same as receiving baptism in the Name of Jesus, it must be taken in faith. From a place of faith, open your mouth and speak what is being stirred in the deepest part of your being. Yield yourself to the LORD.

What Now?

Chapter 22 - Spiritual Warfare

> Finally, my brethren, be strong in the Lord, and in the power of His might. Put on the whole armor of God, that ye may be able to **stand** against the wiles of the devil. For we wrestle not against flesh and blood, but against principalities, against powers, against the rulers of the darkness of this world, against spiritual wickedness in high *places*. Wherefore take unto you the whole armor of God, that ye may be able to **withstand** in the evil day, and having done all, to **stand**. **Stand** therefore, having your loins girt about with truth, and having on the breastplate of righteousness; And your feet shod with the preparation of the gospel of peace; Above all, taking the shield of faith, wherewith ye shall be able to quench all the fiery darts of the wicked. And take the helmet of salvation, and the sword of the Spirit, which is the word of God:
>
> - Ephesians 6:10-17, King James Version (KJV)

In his letter to the Ephesians, Paul writes to the church to identify who, what, and how we fight as we engage in spiritual warfare in our time on the earth. It must first become apparent that we are not engaged with a fight against God. As we have looked throughout the Bible, the picture of God we see is of a merciful and loving God. There is, however, an adversary (the devil) who is challenging God at all points and who seeks to destroy us. In verse 10 above we are edified by Paul to "be strong in the Lord, and in the power of His might." There is strength IN the LORD. Continuing in His Word, spending time in prayerful meditation of His Word, and communing with the Holy Spirit provide for us strength. Moreover, this is not through our power or ability, but through "His might." How good is it to know we are strengthened by the power and ability of the Most High God! Read back over what we have discussed in previous chapters pertaining to God's power and ability, about what we are guaranteed in our covenant with God. These verses from Ephesians start with what we have.

Verse 11 and 12, however, begin to tell us what we as Christians are to do now: "Put on the whole armor of God, that ye may be able to **stand** against the wiles of the devil. For we wrestle not against flesh and blood, but against principalities, against powers, against the rulers of the darkness of this world, against spiritual wickedness in high *places*." We are to put on the "whole armor of God" (more on that later) so that we may "stand." There is a lot of weight behind the use of the word stand. To stand implies that there will be situations that will challenge you. If I were to be encouraging you to stand or take a stand then I would be implying the opportunity to not stand, perhaps to sit or lie down or even to run away. The strength of God, provided to us through His armor, enables us to stand. Stand in storms and peace. Stand in good times and in bad. Stand when others run away.

Compare this to the words of Jesus in Matthew 7:24-27 and Luke 6:46-49, the parable of two builders. When we listen to and build our lives around the Word of God with corresponding action, we are able to stand against the storms of life. Looking back at Ephesians 6:11, our eyes should be drawn to what it is we are to stand against: the wiles of the devil. Not strength, not power. Not some impossible and incomprehensible force. Our God provides more than enough to make up for any lack in our own lives. We however must stand against his "wiles." Peter gives us encouragement on how to do this in 1 Peter 5:6-9 (Berean Standard Bible, BSB):

> Humble yourselves, therefore, under God's mighty hand, so that in due time He may exalt you. Cast all your anxiety on Him, because He cares for you.
>
> Be sober-minded and alert. Your adversary the devil prowls around like a roaring lion, seeking someone to devour. Resist him, standing firm in your faith and in the knowledge that your brothers throughout the world are undergoing the same kinds of suffering.

Notice what Peter is telling us: be humble, submit to God, give your anxieties and cares to God, be clear-minded, and resist the devil. The order of that is important as humility and submission, a mind clear of worldly cares and anxiety are important in resisting the devil. Similarly, James writes in James 4:7-8 (BSB):

> Submit yourselves, then, to God. Resist the devil, and he will flee from you. Draw near to God, and He will draw near to you. Cleanse your hands, you sinners, and purify your hearts, you double-minded.

Just prior to these verses in James and the verses in 1 Peter, both authors actually quote Proverbs 3:34 (Good News Translation, GNT):

> He [God] has no use for conceited people, but shows favor to those who are humble.

A picture should be forming in our minds for how the LORD would have us engage in spiritual warfare. The very first step is in humbling (not belittling) ourselves. Exalt the LORD and rely on His strength. Clear your mind of the things that are troubling you. Do not be double-minded, waffling between action and inaction. Repent from sin and a works-based life. In doing this, you have prepared yourself to face the enemy. But who is our enemy? How does the enemy come? What is intended to be our action?

Chapter 23 - Our Adversary

The answers to each of these can be found in the verse we examined in Ephesians. First, let us examine Ephesians 6:11 in the Amplified Bible (AMP):

> Put on the full armor of God [for His precepts are like the splendid armor of a heavily-armed soldier], so that you may be able to [successfully] stand up against all the schemes *and* the strategies *and* the deceits of the devil.

That word that was translated as "wiles" in the KJV is here translated as "all the schemes *and* the strategies *and* the deceits." The Holman Christian Standard Bible (HCS) uses the word "tactics," both the Contemporary English Version (CEV) and the Good News Translation (GNT) use the word, "tricks." Let us now go back to the beginning, to Genesis 3:1 (BSB):

> Now the serpent was more crafty than any beast of the field that the LORD God had made. And he said to the woman, "Did God really say, 'You must not eat from any tree in the garden?'"

Examine two parts of this text: 1) the serpent is immediately identified as crafty and 2) he came to the woman asking a question. "Did God really say?" What a dangerous question! The Word of God is truth, it is absolute. One must know intimately the Word of God if they are to have success in resisting this adversary. Once the devil (which in the Greek means "slanderous, falsely accusing") has a foothold in your own question of truth or reality, he has the upperhand and he can begin to separate you from God. As we looked at in the first chapter, God has endeavored to bring us back into right relationship with Him. The devil, meanwhile, has endeavored since the beginning to pull us away from God. Consider how the "tempter," another name for the devil, approached Jesus in the desert in Matthew 4:2-4 (BSB):

> After fasting forty days and forty nights, He [Jesus] was hungry.
>
> The tempter came to Him and said, "If You are the Son of God, tell these stones to become bread."
>
> But Jesus answered, "It is written: 'Man shall not live on bread alone, but on every word that comes from the mouth of God.'"

Notice how the devil comes to Jesus not when Jesus is at the height of strength but after He had been fasting and "was hungry." We are the most susceptible to temptation and attacks by the devil when we are at our weakest. That is when he chooses to attack us. The attack is much the same as when he attacked Eve, through questioning what we know from God to be true. Jesus does not need to prove His divinity, especially to a being who has existed much like Jesus has for millenia. God has the power to fulfill a request like the one that the devil is proposing. What then is the issue with what was said? Though Jesus was hungry, there is no benefit to a miracle in turning stones into bread. Miracles are made manifest not to prove divinity but to bring glory and honor to the Divine, the One True God. Who was there to witness the proposed miracle? God made flesh and a fallen angel. Who then would be glorifying God for the completion of this miracle? Certainly not the devil. So we see that the act here is challenging God. It's a bit like saying, "If you really are God, prove it!" In fact, reading further in Matthew 4:5-7 (BSB) we see the following:

> Then the devil took Him to the holy city and set Him on the pinnacle of the temple. "If You are the Son of God," he said, "throw Yourself down. For it is written:
>
> 'He will command His angels concerning You,
> and they will lift You up in their hands,
> so that You will not strike Your foot
> against a stone.'"
>
> Jesus replied, "It is also written: 'Do not put the Lord your God to the test.'"

As He did before, Jesus rebukes the devil. But how He does is so important for us: Jesus uses the Word of God. Now what might be a revelation to believers is that the devil also knows Scripture. Notice how the devil quotes from Psalms, some of the very Psalms that David wrote. Does that mean the devil and David are in cahoots? No! It does, however, show us that the misappropriation and misapplication of Scriptures can lead to that which is not the will of God (consider the Spanish Inquisition, for instance, or the witch burnings in Salem, Massachusetts). The verses above quote Psalm 91:11-12. Psalm 91:1-2 give us the context for these protective verses (BSB):

> He who dwells in the shelter of the Most High will abide in the shadow of the Almighty. I will say to the LORD, "You are my refuge and my fortress, my God, in whom I trust."

The protections in verses 11-12 are attributed to one who dwells in the shelter of the Most High. This is not a person who is testing the LORD but a person who relies upon Him completely. Oh that we would allow ourselves to be dependent upon the LORD like that!

Consider the previous chapter where we read, 1 Peter 5:8 (BSB), "Be sober-minded and alert. Your adversary the devil prowls around like a roaring lion, seeking someone to devour." Our enemy, the devil, has the goal to devour us. Our mind is how he gains access so we are to always be aware that the access he has is what we allow him to have. We must be mindful of how we think, especially when we consider who the devil is.

While imprisoned on the Isle of Patmos, John has a revelation from Jesus. In Revelation 12:10-12 (BSB), we see a glimpse of how satan came to earth:

> "Now have come the salvation and the power
> and the kingdom of our God,
> and the authority of His Christ.
> For the accuser of our brothers has been thrown down—
> he who accuses them day and night before our God.
> They have conquered him by the blood of the Lamb
> and by the word of their testimony.
> And they did not love their lives
> so as to shy away from death.
> Therefore rejoice, O heavens,
> and you who dwell in them!
> But woe to the earth and the sea;
> **with great fury the devil has come down to you,**
> **knowing he has only a short time**."

Notice the bolded statement, the devil knows his time is short. It is not that his power is great, but his fury. Our adversary is clever and furious but his days are numbered. Reading on to the 20th chapter of Revelation, verse 10 (BSB), we can see satan's final resting place, "And the devil who had deceived them was thrown into the lake of fire and sulfur, into which the beast and the false prophet had already been thrown. There they will be tormented day and night forever and ever." Hallelujah! He is a defeated foe! The enemy knows his days are numbered so he will try to deceive you, steal from you, and separate you from the goodness of God. Stay "sober-minded" and know that his days are numbered!

Chapter 24 - Test the Spirits

If we are to be dependent on the LORD then we are to be skeptical of anything that is contrary to Him and His Word. Both Peter and John, two disciples who literally walked the Earth with Jesus, warn us of being led astray. In Matthew 17:1-13, we can read about Jesus going up on a high mountain with Peter, James, and John. Peter cites the experience in 2 Peter 1:16-21 (New American Standard, NAS):

> For we did not follow cleverly devised tales when we made known to you the power and coming of our Lord Jesus Christ, but we were eyewitnesses of His majesty. For when He received honor and glory from God the Father, such a declaration as this was made to Him by the Majestic Glory: "This is My beloved Son with whom I am well pleased"— and we ourselves heard this declaration made from heaven when we were with Him on the holy mountain.

> And *so* we have the prophetic word *made* more sure, to which you do well to pay attention as to a lamp shining in a dark place, until the day dawns and the morning star arises in your hearts. *But* know this first *of all,* that no prophecy of Scripture becomes *a matter* of *someone's* own interpretation, for no prophecy was ever made by an act of human will, but men moved by the Holy Spirit spoke from God.

Peter here identifies that there are prophecies which are legitimately from God. In fact, he states that actual prophecy comes from men "moved by the Holy Spirit" who "spoke from God." In that same sentence, Peter makes it incredibly clear that he first is talking about prophecies in the Bible and our interpretation of them. Peter cautions that while we are to be aware of and pay attention to prophecies, allowing them to be "a lamp shining in a dark place," there must be care in place around interpreting the meaning of said prophecy. Consider verse 20 (AMP), "But understand this first of all, that no prophecy of Scripture is *a matter* of *or* comes from one's own [personal or special] interpretation," noting the importance of someone else helping to derive meaning in the prophecy. Consider Paul's words in 1 Corinthians 14:29-31 (BSB) pertaining to the proper way to hold a church service:

> Two or three prophets should speak, and the others should weigh carefully what is said. And if a revelation comes to someone who is seated, the first speaker should stop. For you can all prophesy in turn so that everyone may be instructed and encouraged.

There is value in prophecy as much as there is revelation about that word of prophecy. It is important, however, to not just use head knowledge but through the Spirit, test words spoken by people, both in and out of church services (yes, test the words of your own pastor/priest to see if the Word of God confirms them!) Look at what Paul wrote to the Galatian church in Galatians 1:6-9 (BSB):

> I am amazed how quickly you are deserting the One who called you by the grace of Christ and are turning to a different gospel— which is not even a gospel. Evidently some people are troubling you and trying to distort the gospel of Christ.
>
> But even if we or an angel from heaven should preach a gospel contrary to the one we preached to you, let him be under a curse! As we have said before, so now I say again: If anyone is preaching to you a gospel contrary to the one you received, let him be under a curse!

Wow! Pronouncing a curse on those who would preach a gospel contrary to the Word of God, that gospel that Paul (as well as Peter) was preaching. Test the words spoken by a "prophet" by the Word of God. Sense in your spirit whether or not there is truth to what is being spoken through revelation by His Spirit. We should be like the Berean church who did not blindly accept what was preached without confirming it in the Scriptures as we can read in Acts 17:11 (New International Version, NIV): "Now the Berean Jews were of more noble character than those in Thessalonica, for they received the message with great eagerness and examined the Scriptures every day to see if what Paul said was true." John acts as a third witness (Peter and Paul were the first two) to how we are to react to words that present themselves as the Word of God in 1 John 4:1-3 (BSB):

> Beloved, do not believe every spirit, but test the spirits to see whether they are from God. For many false prophets have gone out into the world. By this you will know the Spirit of God: Every spirit that confesses that Jesus Christ has come in the flesh is from God, and every spirit that does not confess Jesus is not from God. This is the spirit of the antichrist, which you have heard is coming and which is already in the world at this time.

And again in 1 John 5:9-12 (BSB):

> Even if we accept human testimony, the testimony of God is greater. For this is the testimony that God has given about His Son. Whoever believes in the Son of God has this testimony within him; whoever does not believe God has made Him out to be a liar, because he has not believed in the testimony that God has given about His Son.
>
> And this is that testimony: God has given us eternal life, and this life is in His Son. Whoever has the Son has life; whoever does not have the Son of God does not have life.

How can we know what to trust? How can we know what is true? In the world of theoretical physics and mathematics, calculations and derivations are based on "first principles," in such a way that scientists throw out everything and start with what is known to be true. How do we know it to be "true?" Oftentimes this means not including that which is observed because by observing something has inherently affected it (consider Heisenberg's Uncertainty Principle that dictates a certain amount of uncertainty around measurements of a subatomic particle). For many people, an experience with God happens such that they become intimately aware that He is, though maybe not knowing *who* He is. If we let experience alone shape who God is, we will let negative experiences of religion (not God) taint who we believe God to be. The "first principles" of every Christian should be the Bible and the Witness of the Holy Spirit within them.

Start in your thought life. Take hold of a thought and make a choice with it: grab hold of it or reject it. In this process, bind demonic forces from interfering with your thought life and believe that you will be led by the Spirit of God. From here, monitor your thoughts: do I see the same thought(s) coming up? Consult with the Word of God pertaining to that thought. You may discover a new line of thinking that opens up the revelation of God for you. You may discover that a part of your thinking is actually contrary to the Truth and that you must actively resist it. The Church has, in many areas, allowed bad teaching and religious nonsense to dictate how the Church operates and what the Church teaches for over a thousand years. By not consistently going back to the Word of God, by redefining or misinterpreting what is in the Word of God, or by turning away from the Word of God, man has allowed a twisting and perturbing of what the Church should be. Consider a congregation that talks only of "seed doctrine" but never takes the time to teach on moral excellence. Both are biblical but focusing on one aspect of the Bible such that other principles are neglected would be to the detriment of all congregants. Another example can be in preaching that because we have grace we can act however we want as long as we repent afterwards (some pastors actually teach this). Grace does afford us a life we cannot possibly afford and God will forgive us our sins if we would only repent of them. Purposefully living outside of God's will by refusing to submit to His desire for us (as holy and set apart) can lead us to being open for attack. Walking in sin weakens a person's spiritual defenses and opens them up to the forces of darkness.

Test the spirits yourself by examining your own thought life. What thoughts and mindsets are binding you? Where do you allow yourself to be deceived? What beliefs do you hold tightly to that are based on man's logic instead of God's Truth? We are all attacked daily by demonic spirits on the thought level. You may not be faced each day with the casting out of demons as Jesus was but you are absolutely faced with deciding which spirits guide your thoughts each and every moment of your day. In taking time to check your own heart (residing place of mindsets) and your mind (traffic control of your thoughts) you will find areas to grow spiritually by rejecting that which you know is not of God and allowing those challenging words from God to change you from the inside out (see the section on "What is Repentance?" for a more in-depth discussion of "mind-renewal").

Chapter 25 - Speak the Truth in Love

In this book, we have covered repentance of sin and dead works. We have discussed prayer, tongues, and prophecy. We have addressed what a covenant is and what the church is. We have looked at who our adversary is and how he comes. What now? What are we supposed to do with all of this? How do we take this information and that the first step into the life Jesus has called us to? Let us start with the words the Holy Spirit had Paul write in the fourth chapter of his letter to Ephesus (Ephesians 4:14-16, BSB):

> Then we will no longer be infants, tossed about by the waves and carried around by every wind of teaching and by the clever cunning of men in their deceitful scheming. Instead, **speaking the truth in love**, we will in all things grow up into Christ Himself, who is the head. From Him the whole body, fitted and held together by every supporting ligament, grows and builds itself up in love through the work of each individual part.

Notice in these verses that Paul has identified that these believers are no longer to be as infants, blown about by false teachings (see the previous section). Paul then states that we will "in all things grow up." How? By "speaking the truth in love." He states that the body of us believers grows up "in love through the work of each individual part." Paul gives us a great revelation of the importance of love in 1 Corinthians 13, a chapter referred to as the "love chapter." Most of this chapter is often quoted in marriage ceremonies since the bulk of it is about love. The context however (remember that we've looked at chapters 12 and 14 in depth in previous chapters) pertains to the church service and the proper application of tongues and prophecy. Let us look at all 13 verses of 1 Corinthians 13 (BSB):

> If I speak in the tongues of men and of angels, but have not love, I am only a ringing gong or a clanging cymbal. If I have the gift of prophecy and can fathom all mysteries and all knowledge, and if I have absolute faith so as to move mountains, but have not love, I am nothing. If I give all I possess to the poor and exult in the surrender of my body, but have not love, I gain nothing.

> Love is patient, love is kind. It does not envy, it does not boast, it is not proud. It is not rude, it is not self-seeking, it is not easily angered, it keeps no account of wrongs. Love takes no pleasure in evil, but rejoices in the truth. 7It bears all things, believes all things, hopes all things, endures all things.

> Love never fails. But where there are prophecies, they will cease; where there are tongues, they will be restrained; where there is knowledge, it will be dismissed. For

we know in part and we prophesy in part, but when the perfect comes, the partial passes away.

When I was a child, I talked like a child, I thought like a child, I reasoned like a child. When I became a man, I set aside childish ways. Now we see but a dim reflection as in a mirror; then we shall see face to face. Now I know in part; then I shall know fully, even as I am fully known.

And now these three remain: faith, hope, and love; but the greatest of these is love.

The gifts of tongues, prophecy, and acts of incredible giving are all without merit from a person without love. What a powerful statement! Recall our early chapters when we discussed repentance. A person who does not have love in their hearts yet gives prophecies or speaks and interprets other tongues or gives of their time and resources needs to repent! How can that be? It is because these works are just that, works, when they are not done for the glory of God. How can God be glorified in actions without love? It is not the actions that God seeks: He is looking for the love and adoration of His people. Moreover, this is the same love and adoration that we are to show *each other*!

In his letter, James writes of the importance of tending to our words (James 1:26, Aramaic Bible in Plain English), "And if a man thinks that he serves God, and does not hold his tongue, but deceives his heart, this person's service is worthless." He gives us further insight in James 3:2-12 (BSB):

We all stumble in many ways. If anyone is never at fault in what he **says**, he is a perfect man, able to control his whole body.

When we put bits into the mouths of horses to make them obey us, we can guide the whole animal. Consider ships as well. Although they are so large and are driven by strong winds, they are steered by a very small rudder wherever the pilot is inclined.

In the same way, the **tongue** is a small part of the body, but it boasts of great things. Consider how small a spark sets a great forest ablaze. The **tongue** also is a fire, a world of wickedness among the parts of the body. It pollutes the whole person, sets the course of his life on fire, and is itself set on fire by hell.

All kinds of animals, birds, reptiles, and creatures of the sea are being tamed and have been tamed by man, but no man can tame the **tongue**. It is a restless evil, full of deadly poison.

With the **tongue** we bless our Lord and Father, and with it we curse men, who have been made in God's likeness. Out of the same **mouth** come blessing and cursing. My brothers, this should not be! Can both fresh water and salt water flow from the same spring? My brothers, can a fig tree grow olives, or a grapevine bear figs? Neither can a salt spring produce fresh water.

Through his use of figurative language, James paints a picture of our difficulty with our own tongue. Consider verse 9, "With the tongue we bless our Lord and Father, and with it we curse men, who have been made in God's likeness." This is one of the largest fields of battle we face now and will ever face: the battle for control of our tongue. Solomon writes about the tongue in Proverbs 18. Consider verses 4, 6-8, 13, 15, 17, 20-21:

> The words of a man's **mouth** are deep waters;
> the fountain of wisdom is a bubbling brook.

> A fool's **lips** bring him strife,
> and his **mouth** invites a beating.

> A fool's **mouth** is his ruin,
> and his **lips** are a snare to his soul.

> The **words** of a gossip are like choice morsels
> that go down into the inmost being.

> He who answers a matter before he **hears** it—
> this is folly and disgrace to him.

> The heart of the discerning acquires knowledge,
> and the **ear** of the wise seeks it out.

> The first to **state** his case seems right
> until another comes and cross-examines him.

> From the fruit of his **mouth** a man's belly is filled;
> with the harvest from his **lips** he is satisfied.

> Life and death are in the power of the **tongue**,
> and those who love it will eat its fruit.

Notice the comparisons of the impact of the speaking and hearing of words. The last verse quoted is one most often quoted when a bit of sage advice is needed about speaking the right words. Take time and read through each of these verses a few times.

What sticks out? What rings true? What is something new? Do any of these seem contrary to wisdom? Solomon was known as the wisest man who ever lived. Perhaps we should take in this godly wisdom and let it lead to a change in us.

There is an old children's rhyme that goes like this: "Sticks and stones may break my bones but words will never hurt me." We should know through our study that this is an absolute lie! Words have incredible power and to negate that is absolutely contrary to the Bible. Consider our earlier section on prayer and the importance of "saying." As Christians, we can not simply speak the words others around us say. We must instead speak words of faith, words that support (not contradict) the Bible. Think about sayings like "I'm scared to death!" Are you? How about the more recent saying when someone thinks something is funny: "I'm dead." Are you? We must consider the fruit we will reap when we continually say the same words a corrupt and hurting world uses. We must more carefully choose our words, or at the very least quit being mad at God when we reap from those words!

Our words create our future. Each is a seed that will produce a harvest. There is little we can do about the harvest that we have already planted. We can of course work to root out that which is planted by examining the mindset we have allowed to take place in our hearts but in the end we will reap what we sow. We can, however, work to change what the next season of crops will look like. We can speak "life" over a situation: "I speak life and peace over my city" instead of "this town is going to hell in a hand-basket." We can stop agreeing with people who are speaking words of death just to be pleasant and cordial: "All of these politicians are corrupt and beyond saving," regardless of your political beliefs, you are called to speak against the corrupting spirits, not the people. We are to use our words as a weapon by pulling down imaginations and everything that exalts itself against the authority and lordship of Christ: "My child/wife/husband/business is my everything and my life would have no meaning without them," should quickly be replaced with, "I give glory to God that He has given me my child/wife/husband/business. I know that even if I were to lose them, I would not lose my God." Jesus reminds us in Luke 6:45 where the source of our words lies (BSB): "The good man brings good things out of the good treasure of his heart, and the evil man brings evil things out of the evil treasure of his heart. For out of the overflow of the heart, the mouth speaks." Therefore, we endeavor to let mind renewal happen each and everyday, allowing for the change in our hearts as well as the corresponding changing of our words. Even non-believers understand the importance of words (the field of "positive psychology" correlates mindsets and words used to success). What separates the believer in this regard is that we do not have to guess what caused the success of a person. We can see that when people allow their words to be God's words, it produces success every time! Consider Psalm 19:14, NLT, "May the words of my mouth and the meditation of my heart be pleasing to you, O LORD, my rock and my redeemer." Do not forget Proverbs 4:4, BSB, '...he taught me and said,

"Let your heart lay hold of my words; keep my commands and you will live."' Or the LORD's guidance in Deuteronomy 11:18, BSB, "Fix these words of mine in your hearts and minds; tie them as reminders on your hands and bind them on your foreheads." Know the Word of God and proclaim it! Let us examine Ephesians 5:15-20 (BSB) to draw upon the wisdom imparted to Paul that he shares with the church in Ephesus:

> Pay careful attention, then, to how you walk, not as unwise but as wise, redeeming the time, because the days are evil. Therefore do not be foolish, but understand what the Lord's will is. Do not get drunk on wine, which leads to reckless indiscretion. Instead, be filled with the Spirit.
>
> **Speak to one another** with psalms, hymns, and spiritual songs. Sing and make music in your hearts to the Lord, always giving thanks to God the Father for everything in the name of our Lord Jesus Christ.

In addition to his guidance to not act like the people around them, Paul advises that the believers would speak to each other in peaceable ways through psalms, hymns, and spiritual songs. Our words should be a demonstration of the love of God flowing through us. We are to fight our spiritual fight in the same way Jesus did: with our words. In Ephesians 6 we are reminded of this as Paul outlines the "spiritual equipment the believer should have equipped, concluding with (6:17, BSB), "...the sword of the Spirit, which is the word of God." Renew your mind to the promises God outlines in His Word and you will find yourself living from the place of His grace. Read through Ephesians 1 and notice all of the places Paul draws attention to "praising the glory" of God. Meditate on the chapter and see what revelation it brings you about the good things God has in store for you!

As we conclude this final section, we are to be mindful of what the LORD is calling us to do, love the LORD your God and each other, resist the devil, and speak words of life into this hurting world. In John's gospel account, Jesus speaks these words (John 13:34-35, BSB): "A new commandment I give you: Love one another. As I have loved you, so you also must love one another. By this everyone will know that you are My disciples, if you love one another." We are to be the Christian that is known as a disciple of Jesus of Nazareth, not because we say we are but because the words we choose to use and the way we express love to each other should tell of who we are. Let us offer a prayer to help us on our journey to be a greater witness to Christ:

> Father God in Heaven, all glory and honor is Yours! We thank You that You sent us Jesus and showed us how to live godly lives. Father, we ask for the strength and wisdom to continue in the way You have shown us, to continually resist the devil and refuse to compromise in speaking words of truth and of life. We recommit

ourselves in every moment of stumbling to be a beacon of light and hope in a hurting world. We will be known as Your followers not by grand acts or loud words but by the love You have taught us. Father, reveal to us Your love in a greater way not for our own benefit but to share with others so we may cause others to glorify You. May Your Spirit guide us in all truth today. We thank You for hearing our prayers in the wonderful Name of Jesus. Amen.

Life is full of choices. Seek out the Word of God for any situation and pray for guidance such that the Holy Spirit residing within you will give a divine revelation about your situation. Ask and you shall receive, knock and the door will be open. The LORD provides for His people. Seek Him earnestly, believing that He will reward you and you will not be in lack.

Conclusion

May your journey be one filled with growth that brings you closer to God. I pray that this book will help and not be a hindrance to anyone on this walk of life. Set time aside to pray and meditate on His Word to receive from Him the next steps He has for you. Perhaps He has already spoken these words to you and it is time to follow His lead. Wherever you are in your relationship with God, know that I love you and I am praying for you to know more deeply what it is God has for you.

Below are each of the prayers the LORD helped me to draft. I pray that you will find your own way to pray. Until then, feel free to use these as a guide to give the glory to the Almighty and ask for His involvement in Your life in a biblical way.

Consider the following prayer and let it aid you as you practice repentance:

> LORD God in Heaven, how great is Your mercy and goodness! I thank You for sending Jesus of Nazareth down to earth to be the one time sacrifice for my sins. I invite you to work in me through Your Holy Spirit. Examine my thoughts and my mind, search out the deepest places of my heart. Help me to see where I have missed You or have fallen off the straight path you have laid before me. Show me where in my life unforgiveness is holding me back so that I may forgive others and myself for no other reason than to bring glory to Your Name. I am no longer the old creature but a new creation in Christ. I make a no turning back decision to be led by You and Your Spirit from this day forward. I soften my heart to You and humbly seek to serve you in a deeper way today. It is in the Name of the LORD Jesus Christ, I pray, Amen.

Affirm your covenant with the Almighty God with this prayer:

> Father God in Heaven, how great is Your Name! You sent Jesus down with a most holy Name so that I would be redeemed from death and destruction. How merciful is my LORD! How worthy He is to be praised! I say thank you for Jesus and I ask that you reveal to my spirit a greater knowledge of Your covenant with me for I have a covenant with the Most High God. Show me all of Your mercies. Show me all of Your goodness. By faith I take my healing, it is my right. By faith I take restoration of finances, it is my right. I am forgiven not because I am worthy but because you are good. The Blood of Jesus, my LORD, purifies me so that I may

better serve my God. All glory and honor is Yours, Almighty Father, forever and ever. It is in the Name of Your Son, Jesus I pray. Amen.

Our prayer then should be for us to be taught of God the best way we can demonstrate this grace to the world around us:

Almighty Father, how gracious are You! You have freely given me a life I could never deserve through Jesus, Your Son. I thank You for calling me to You and I accept this calling. Today, I endeavor to not back down from the darkness in this present world but to present the Light that is Jesus to it. May my life be a story that tells of your goodness and mercy. LORD, guide me today so that I may forgive those that hurt me, even myself. Show me now where unforgiveness is in my heart so that I may forgive and turn back to You. Guide me so that I would let the love You have shown me radiate out from me to this hurting world. Father, I say "yes" to the work You have called me to. I speak the Name of Jesus over hurting situations because I believe that the same power that saved me and brought me to wholeness will bring wholeness to others. I pray "shalom," nothing missing, nothing broken, over this nation and the people in it. In the coming days, show me more of You and Your grace in action so that in turn I may share it with the world! In the Mighty Name of Jesus I pray, amen.

Meditating on our discussion of who the Christian is and their responsibility in these the last days, let us pray for guidance:

Father God in heaven, Your mercy endures forever! We pray that our joy and the joy of our fellow believers would be full, as it is our strength. We pray that those in authority, elected, appointed, or promoted would hear and heed the Word of God for it brings light and revelation. We pray that Your Hand be upon them, guiding and directing their decisions. Father, we welcome You into our hearts to stir a deeper revelation for what gifts You have given us. We ask that Your Holy Spirit which indwells us brings forth words to say as we pray and intercede for this hurting world around us. Open our eyes to the role You have for us in this world so that we may live and operate more fully in Your Will. All praise and glory are Yours, Almighty Father. It is in the blessed Name of Jesus we pray. Amen.

When a person is born again by making Jesus Christ the LORD of their life, Jesus sends His Spirit to reside on the inside of you. All born-again believers have the Holy Spirit already so there is no need to pray for Him. If you have not received the baptism of the Holy Spirit as evidenced by speaking in other tongues, pray this prayer and commit yourself to allowing the Spirit of God to speak through you:

Father God, I believe with all of my heart that Jesus is the one way to You. I make Him the LORD of every aspect of my life and submit fully to Him. I receive now, through Your rich grace, the baptism of the Holy Spirit. I release Him to speak through my mouth and my vocal chords, speaking in languages known and unknown. I will not question or challenge the Holy Spirit but will confirm the words and works spoken by the Word of God. I thank You LORD that through Jesus Christ, You count me worthy. I say now lips be loosed in the Name of Jesus. I speak now with my spirit and not with my mind. I glorify the Father for the gift of the Holy Spirit. I glorify God for His infinite grace. Thank you LORD. In Jesus Name I pray. Amen.

Let us offer a prayer to help us on our journey to be a greater witness to Christ:

Father God in Heaven, all glory and honor is Yours! We thank You that You sent us Jesus and showed us how to live godly lives. Father, we ask for the strength and wisdom to continue in the way You have shown us, to continually resist the devil and refuse to compromise in speaking words of truth and of life. We recommit ourselves in every moment of stumbling to be a beacon of light and hope in a hurting world. We will be known as Your followers not by grand acts or loud words but by the love You have taught us. Father, reveal to us Your love in a greater way not for our own benefit but to share with others so we may cause others to glorify You. May Your Spirit guide us in all truth today. We thank You for hearing our prayers in the wonderful Name of Jesus. Amen.

Appendix - Tongues, Travailing, and Psalms

Tongues

As described in Scripture, "tongues" will come in two primary "sounds," speaking in a foreign tongue (foreign to the speaker, but not the listener) and speaking in an unknown tongue (referred to as an "angelic language"). There are many examples given by people who had gotten up in front of people and began speaking about Jesus in a language or dialect they did not know yet they were very much understood by those around. The example of this form of speaking in tongues is given by the Day of Pentecost when the other Jews around accused the disciples of being "drunk." Have you ever known someone who got drunk and then was able to speak in a language they did not know? That is exactly the accusation made that day. This sign from God was powerful enough that 5000 accepted Jesus Christ as their LORD and were saved.

The second form of speaking or praying in tongues is the form most people refute, praying in an "unknown tongue." How do you pray in something "unknown?" On this point, I will speak from my own experience (as Chapter 19 details much of what the Bible says on these kinds of tongues). Raised Catholic, I have been to a variety of church services: Sunday services, Feast Day services, Youth Group services, and the occasional weekday service. In many of these services, there were times of "silent prayer" as well as times of corporate praying or praising. There are two particular types of service that I would say stood out to me: the Stations of the Cross (on Good Friday, the Church gathers to recall the suffering Jesus went through on His way to and through the crucifixion) and Adoration will on youth retreats (the Eucharist or Body of Christ is placed in a golden stand of sorts so it can be seen by the congregation in a time of prayer and praise).

In reflection on the suffering of Jesus at the Stations of the Cross, there is this emotion of grief at the suffering of this man: suffering as a sinner not because He sinned but because we all have sinned. In those moments, one considers the price paid at each stop, the little interactions of people along the way. See yourself as Pontius Pilate, failing to understand why the Jews would rather have a murderer released than the kind and mild Jesus who stood before him. See yourself as the soldiers placing the heavy cross on the shoulders of Jesus. See yourself as Mary, the mother of Jesus, coming face-to-face with Jesus after He falls the first time. See yourself as Simon of Cyrene, a bystander forced to help Jesus carry the cross. See yourself as the women to whom Jesus said, "Weep not for me but for you and your children." See yourself as the men driving nails into the hands and feet of Jesus. Through this time in contemplation of the suffering of Jesus, one comes into contact with what Jesus paid. Salvation seems all the more valuable when you know the price paid. This example (though absent from any praying in tongues) has value because at times it may be accompanied by a heaviness so to speak (we will mention again when we discuss "travailing"). One starts to glimpse the "compassion" Jesus often spoke about that moved Him to do mighty deeds.

In the time of Adoration, there is a lightness. The focus is on Jesus, not His brutal murder. In particular, I still have in my mind a time at a youth retreat where we had gathered before the Sacrament of the Eucharist (the bread that is blessed and taken as a remembrance of the Covenant Meal with Jesus before His crucifixion) and the youth leader was leading us in a time of worship. While singing and praising God, this powerful emotion hit me: an awe that literally brought me to tears. It was an experience I was unfamiliar with and caught me unaware. It put in my mind the image of bowing before the Most High God. I had the very real sense that this is not just some ritualistic practice but that God is truly glorified in these moments of a couple dozen youth gathered in a dark room singing praises to Him.

While there were no "tongues" present in either event, these emotional and spiritual experiences have a sensation that connects with experiences of "praying in the Spirit." My first experience with tongues was at the house of my in-laws in Rio Rancho before Michaella and I were married. I had found my way back to the LORD and I was starting to go to church again. We gathered in the living room to pray over my mother in-law and as we all extended our hands, I could hear my wife and father in-law praying, they would alternate between words in English and something else, as far as I could tell. The words flowed out in an astonishing way, sometimes repeating certain sounds or phrases. It took on the nature of Farsi (Persian) or Greek, some letter sound combinations familiar, some unique. Over the next few months I would find myself listening to Kenneth Hagin or Creflo A. Dollar or some other more "charismatic" preacher and at times I would hear them pray in this similar way. A variety of prayers, a variety of contexts, decades apart in time, all with a similar sound in prayer.

I remember sitting in Michaella's apartment with her one night, troubled by the declining mental state of my grandmother. We had been drinking and I was sobbing. We set out to pray for my grandmother and Michaella had encouraged me to pray in the Spirit, from my belly. As I was praying in English, I had this warm sensation stirring just above my belly button. I started with "Hallelujah" multiple times before it gave way to what felt like words pushing themselves out of my mouth. I felt as though the words gushed out of my mouth, no longer held back by my intellect. A sense of joy came over me after some time of praying in this manner.

In following weeks, I would set out to pray in this manner, from the source of my belly, often inhibited by my thinking. "Is this how it should sound?" would rise up in my mind, jumbling the words. The more I took the quiet time to pray, the more the words flowed forth with ease. In time, I would spend upwards of 15 minutes praying, not knowing a single word that was prayed!

As it is now, the LORD may impress me to burst into tongues when a need arises at a moment's notice (some situations I know about, others are simply an inner leading that there is a need). I know of some prayer warriors who dedicate an hour or more everyday to praying in the Spirit. There are those who never pray more than 5 minutes straight in tongues but do so throughout the day. Ephesians 6:18 (BSB) tells us to "Pray in the Spirit at all times, with every kind of prayer and petition." Prayer becomes a lifestyle the more you practice it.

Interpretation

The Bible tells us that when we pray in tongues, we are to ask the Holy Spirit to give us interpretation (1 Corinthians 14:13). I continued to pray in short bursts, on my way to work, after Sunday lunch with my wife's family, in quiet time where I could find it. I noticed in corporate prayer after Sunday lunch I would find that as we would pray in the Spirit, certain people or events would come up in my mind. There was this sensation that the Holy Spirit would lead us to pray over certain people or topics. The truest sense for me would be when a person or subject is brought to my mind and someone else would start praying in English what I was thinking. There was this unity of spirit when we prayed together.

Certain prayer targets had a "weight" to them. Even if the topic was not mentioned beforehand, when a certain topic came up, we could all sense a heaviness loom as we would pray about a topic. After a period of time, that pressure would give way. Sometimes it would just be as though cloud was in the room but sense parted. Other times mid sentence, you would find yourself laughing or giggling. The LORD is not as serious as theologians make Him out to be. Consider the words of Jesus in Matthew 18:3 (BSB), ""Truly I tell you," He said, "unless you change and become like little children, you will never enter the kingdom of heaven." Little children are full of laughter and are not serious by nature. Laughing in prayer was not something I had ever heard of growing up but became commonplace as we set ourselves in the spiritual warfare of praying in the Spirit. The laughter brought with it a sense that not only had the LORD heard my prayers, those prayers were coming to pass in that moment.

The sensation of being guided to pray for someone or some event and the laughter that would accompany "praying through" a prayer topic were the beginnings of having revelation and insight about what it is I was praying about. On my way to work one morning in 2021, I was praying in the Spirit and I asked the LORD for the interpretation of what I was praying. As I was coming up to my exit, the following idea, though not exactly these words, formed in my mind, "Do not pray for revival, for it is happening now in the hearts and minds of My people. The question is whether or not they will step into it." I would meditate on this for the next few weeks. I had just finished listening to the Southwest Believers' Convention and revival was a prominent topic. The great moves of God had been dependent on the faith of those involved. The people must allow that faith to work. There is not some special anointing people need from God in these last days. Instead, the Church must allow the anointing of the Holy Spirit to flow out from itself to others.

A short while later (November 11, 2021), I took time to put my nose to the carpet and pray. I had heard that this was something great prayer warriors do and I earnestly desired to grow in my prayer life. I began praying in the Spirit for about 20 minutes and I asked the LORD to reveal to me His will, to show revelation to me. I continued to pray in the Spirit with my heart fully engaged and I would open my mouth and say these words:

"Speak My words - 'In the beginning was the Word and the Word was with God and the Word was God.' '... and God said, "Light, be," and light was.' Speak light into the people. A time is coming and is now for a culling, a calling. A time of action, to speak My Words into being. My people will separate themselves by speaking light and life.

I have need of you to be a teacher. Your time of idle and profane words must come to an end. You must speak My Words.

Study this out before you seek My Word further."

Even now as I write this, the following verse wells up from within me, "... out of the abundance of the heart, the mouth speaketh." (Matthew 12:34, KJV). God's callings are not without consequence. One cannot be called into purpose or granted power without the means to control that power. I had spent years filling myself up with filth and letting it flow right out. My heart was filled to overflowing with the things of the world. To be used by God, I would need to mind my words. To do that, I would need to clear out the filth I had filled myself with and replace it with the Word of God. My mind would come back to this when I would join in with someone talking poorly about a student or family or situation. I would start to immediately have the thought, "wait a minute, I do not actually agree with that." I would start to feel gross the moment I let curse words leave my mouth. Little by little, the LORD was helping me to embody His Word: I was not only speaking the Word of God, I was living it. This revelation was a personal one. At the same time, however, it is also a universal one. The LORD has called all of us to speak His Word, to be a light to a dark and hurting world.

Travailing

In July of 2023, I was in Atlanta, Georgia for Relay's National Principal Academy. After some of the sessions, I sought to relax and listen to some preaching. A YouTube link with the title, "The secret to a successful apostolic ministry" caught my eye. Over the course of an hour, Kenneth Hagin speaks from personal experience and from the Word about the apostolic ministry (recall that the five-fold ministry is apostles, prophets, evangelists, pastors, and preachers/teachers, Ephesians 4:11). Hagin details a word of knowledge given to him back on December 1, 1948, "Full of faith and power (Holy Ghost) using the divine given instruments of travail and compassion will make you irresistible." These divine instruments stood out to me as I had been drawn to the compassion of Christ and was familiar with it but I knew nothing of travail.

The King James Version of the Bible uses the word "travail" in 65 places throughout the Old and New Testaments. We see in Genesis 35:16 and 38:27 that "travail" is used in conjunction with a pregnancy. Exodus 18:8 and Numbers 20:14 use the word in lieu of "hardships." Psalm 7:14 (BSB) gives an interesting usage, "Behold, the wicked man travails with evil; he conceives trouble and births falsehood." In this verse, we see travail as "pregnant with" but it can easily be seen to also be a "hardship." How can hardship be a tool? Isaiah 42:14 (BSB) shows us the following, "I have kept silent from ages past; I have remained quiet and restrained. But now I will groan like a woman in labor (travail); I will at once gasp and pant." So groaning in travail becomes one such tool. Travail paints a picture of suffering, of hardship, yet with something produced on the other side.

Consider Jesus in the eleventh chapter of John after Lazarus died. Jesus encounters Mary, the sister of Lazarus, and verse 33 (KJV) gives, "When Jesus therefore saw her weeping, and the Jews also weeping which came with her, He groaned in the spirit, and was troubled…" Jesus groans in the Spirit, gives thanks to God, and then calls Lazarus out of the tomb. Jesus, travails with the people, producing forth the resurrection of Lazarus. We can see Paul similarly expressing this "travailing" to the benefit of the church in Galatia, Galatians 4:19 (BSB), "My children, for whom I am again in the pains of childbirth (travail) until Christ is formed in you…" We see Paul in pain, suffering until Christ (the revelation of who He is and what His anointing does) is formed in them. This suffering on the behalf of others through travailing is the tool the Holy Spirit was talking to Kenneth Hagin about.

Compassion

The second tool mentioned was "compassion." In a parable in Matthew 18, Jesus is teaching about a man who is in a lot of debt to his master. Verse 27 (BSB) gives, "His master had compassion on him, forgave his debt, and released him." The master's compassion spared the man in debt, breaking the obligation of it and freeing him from prison. We can see that compassion acted out in Matthew 20:34 when Jesus lays hands on blind men to heal them (BSB): "Moved with compassion, Jesus touched their eyes, and at once they received their sight and followed Him." We also see compassion at work in the multiplication of the loaves and fish in Matthew 15:32 (BSB), "Then Jesus called His disciples to Him and said, "I have compassion for this crowd, because they have already been with Me three days and have nothing to eat. I do not want to send them away hungry, or they may faint along the way." " Matthew 9:34-36 gives a powerful revelation into compassion:

But the Pharisees said, "It is by the prince of demons that He drives out demons." Jesus went through all the towns and villages, teaching in their synagogues, preaching the gospel of the kingdom, and healing every disease and sickness. When He saw the crowds, He was moved with compassion for them, because they were harassed and helpless, like sheep without a shepherd.

The people at the time had religious leaders and teachers (the Pharisees in fact were a prominent group of such teachers). Yet Jesus described the people as "harassed and helpless, like sheep without a shepherd." Compassion is not a religious obligation but a deep caring about people. Jesus intimately cared for the people. In the same way, if we are to see the "greater works" that Jesus charged us with bringing about, we would have to embody the same form of compassion He did.

The next sections detail the experiences I have had with travailing in the Spirit. Student names are represented by an initial to protect their identity.

Intercessory Travailing - July 20, 2023

Around 10:15 PM, I sat down to pray in the Spirit, endeavoring to travail in the Spirit, interceding in a way I never have before. As I prayed, I could sense a leading towards "loss," as though someone had lost a loved one. I could sense a sorrow grip my heart, but as I approached, I began to laugh and peace began to settle. I continued my prayer on the floor until I felt the need to change my position. Around 11 PM I took my watch off to become unencumbered as I continued my time in prayer. A different sensation came upon me, hunger. I found myself calling out, "hungry" and I pursued this into a deepening sense of loss and lack. I began to sob, crying out as one who is starving, desperate for their pleas to be heard. "Won't anybody hear me?" I could hear myself cry. So desperate. I sensed in my spirit further that this was not a physical hunger but spiritual. I then felt myself calling for the Father, "Oh God. I am so hungry, don't forsake me." This desperate sobbing and crying ultimately gave way to the most delightful laughter and a calling out in thanks to the Father. As I sighed deeply in relief, I experienced a great sense of peace. Even as I write, I am calm but a bit shaky. I only travailed from about 11:01-11:18 yet I am more spiritually spent from that time than the 45 minutes of praying prior.

In my spirit, I sense this experience represents many people today. A people so desperate for the LORD, crying out. The sorrow, the lack of purpose, the burden, I nearly go back into sobbing just thinking about it. This must be compassion as I have not known it. I will endeavor to take more time in the future to travail (though this is definitely not the kind of praying you can do in public).

7/20/23 - 11:32 PM EDT

Atlanta, GA

Intercessory Travailing - August 25, 2023

Around 8:13 PM, as I am listening to Keith Moore's praise session from the 2023 Believer's Convention (8.1.23, session 2), he spends a lot of time singing and repeating the phrase, "I'm free." As I sit on the ground listening, my mind is brought to a gentleman who recently had come by to pick up his grandson from school in the parent pick-up line. Having cut the line, parking illegally and yelling profanities at me as I endeavor to keep his grandson out of the way of traffic, I am thinking of how I would respond should he swing at me. As I play through the scenarios, I am quickened to the realization this is a "flesh" reaction, not a spirit reaction. As I turn from the thought of fighting him, a heaviness is felt in my belly, around the region of my diaphragm, I am moved in the Spirit to tears with the overwhelming compassion for this man. In crying and groaning in the Spirit, travailing turns to revelation: there is a panic, a fear due to a trauma in his life. His unforgiveness is burdening him and holding him back. I pray that the eyes of his understanding would be open and that he would feel, in that moment, the warm embrace of the Agape love of Abba, Father. I see myself in the Spirit embrace this man. Slowly, peace sets in.

As I continue to pray in the Spirit, I sense the LORD has more to reveal. Over a period of time, what initially felt as a sharp spike in the heart (a dart, perhaps) becomes a cold hand over the heart, gripping, constricting. It is revealed as the sensation of fear. I am moved with compassion for two students, J. and L., who each, separately, have been attacked by adult strangers in the last week. I can see them with the pained look of fear and trauma. However, through this fear, I can see the joy of the LORD well up within that same heart, warming it until it is free from the bonds of fear and trauma. In a moment of peace, I sit silently, reclined back.

The last vision is of a small child, curled up, cold and alone. I do not travail but am led to pray for those who have nothing. No hope. The LORD reveals that before discussing goals (it has been my target to address "goal-setting" with the students), the kids need to learn to hope. Then they hope, the kids in turn will teach their families to hope. Once they know hope, we can begin to instill the principles of faith! Glory to God for His revelations! Glory to God for His divine mercy!

8/25/25 - 8:52 PM MDT

Albuquerque, New Mexico

Intercessory Travailing - September 1, 2023

At 8:13 AM, I set forth to pray in the Spirit and to travail on the floor in my office at home. I begin by praying and opening myself to what the Spirit of God has for me today. As I move into the spirit, I sense a loss, perhaps of a parent. It becomes clear that it is a loss of a mother. Groaning in the Spirit produces the understanding that the loss experienced is brought on by choice: a mother caught in the cycle of addiction. In the Spirit, I am at one time or another as a child between the ages of 1 and 10, longing for their mother. "It's not fair," I cry out, "come back, mommy." There is a deep sorrow but also a frustration. The inability to do anything about it, just longing for a mother's embrace. As peace begins to settle, I pray for the mothers of J. and M. Both boys have experienced separation from their mother due to drug abuse.

I know the Spirit has more to reveal so I continue to pray. I see my children in the gymnasium, all 460 of them. These are my kids. The love of God washes over me as I think of all of them. Then, suddenly, constriction. I feel a twisting of my body, stopping my breathing. As I gasp and pant, I realize this is anxiety that is gripping my children. A crippling panic and fear that twists and contorts. My body is so very tense, every muscle is tight and I have to think to breathe. I am praying for L., J., J., A., V., and I. I know there are others. I can sense a warmth, a hug, an embrace going forth to all of my kids. I praise the LORD, filling my Spirit back up for I am so empty after the travailing. I am satisfied to know the LORD's work is done in these moments of intercession, I must be mindful to fill myself back up through praise.

9/01/23 - 8:53 AM MDT

Albuquerque, New Mexico

A Psalm Unto the LORD: Spiritual Warfare

A wise man surrounds himself continually with his right-standing with God; it is his shield.

Boldness in authority, tempered by humility of heart, the believing one leads the charge.

"Charge forth, My emissary, My child. I have called you into battle for such a time as this,

Do not fear your enemy, there is victory in the Name of the LORD!

Even the demons tremble before the Name of Jesus!

Forge ahead with the sword of the Spirit in your hand.

Gain ground for My kingdom. The gates of hell will not prevail!

Hell shudders at the Name of Jesus!"

I tremble at the Word of the LORD, but I take strength in Him.

Just as others have stood steadfast in the Name of the LORD, so shall I!

Knowledge of His Word brings comfort. Understanding of His ways brings *Shalom*.

Let my heart not be troubled evermore.

My refuge, my deliverer is with me.

No longer will I back away from Your orders. I will be willing and obedient.

Only the LORD can provide for me in my time of need,

Protecting me from what lies in waiting.

Quieting my heart so that I learn from Him produces understanding; He does not withhold wisdom.

Righteousness is His breastplate, faith is His shield. I put my whole trust in Him.

Shielding me from the fiery darts of the enemy, the *Agape* love of the Father envelopes me.

There is a peace and a calm that defies all understanding.

Under Your grace and Your protection, LORD, I lack nothing.

Victory was had at the cross. The enemy no longer will be lord over me.

With worship and praise, I exalt the victor!

Exalt the Name of the LORD!

Yahweh has given us an everlasting covenant in the Blood of the Lamb.

Zealous is the one who takes hold of the Blood and the victory therein.

6/26/23

Lake City, Colorado

A Psalm Unto the LORD: Salvation in a Time of Need

What is this? Am I to be trapped here? In a desolate wasteland, far from everything, no sign of help. Frustration and anger try to come in, hope diminishing.

In the physical: the impossible before me. The temptation to complain arises.

Instead, we seek you. When I am weak, You are strong! I cast this care, this burden over to You. In Your peace, hope burns.

We are not alone in hearing Your voice: a divine appointment! Helping hands and joyful smiles, the right tools at the right time.

Bless the LORD, O my soul! How good is our God! How great is His mercy!

You bring us out of the desert; out in the wilderness we no longer remain. Your mercy carries us all of the way home. Your joy stirs in our hearts.

How grateful we are to the One True God! The LORD's timing is always perfection, His *checed* is always renewed. How I have learned that the LORD will hear the prayers of His people! He will use the godly to bring forth His blessings and mercy.

I will not complain, lest in the desolate place I would remain. Instead, I will praise the glory of the LORD! I will exalt the Name of Jesus, my victor, my savior.

7/01/23

Albuquerque, New Mexico

Made in the USA
Columbia, SC
08 February 2025